COLLISION COURS

COLLISION COURSE

ROY BROWN

Andersen Press
London

First published in 1980 by
Andersen Press Limited
in association with
Hutchinson Limited,
3 Fitzroy Square,
London, W1

ISBN 0 905478 75 4

Printed in Great Britain

1

During this new phase of his long illness, Green was nursed in a private room—one of the more privileged facilities at the hospital's observation unit.

His seriously impaired memory, and the uneven pattern of his sleeping and waking, gave him no grasp of time sequence: he did not remember when he had arrived, how many days or weeks had elapsed, nor the reason for his presence there. For Green, the sickness had neither diagnosis or prognosis; nor did times and events beyond the confines of his small, white prison have any bearing on its beginning.

Only rarely did Green, lying alone on his bed, give fragmentary thought to his situation. Even then—certainly at first—he did so with utter detachment, feeling no anxiety, nor more than a token curiosity. It was as if his mind brooded over the surface of a dark and stagnant pool and only occasionally would a brief bubble burst out of its depths.

A question, perhaps: *why don't I get any visitors?* But never an extension, a pursuit. Not, for instance: *what* visitors? *Who?*

And there were half-dreams, mostly upon waking out of a drugged sleep: himself, Green, crawling in a labyrinth of underground caves, probing with a weak torch beam into cavities and crevices, his own breath panting and sighing against stone walls. Or sometimes he was floating in a balloon through dense swirling cloud. Memories would strike his face like scorching sun rays, only to vanish swiftly. They revealed no more than images of childhood, or bits read in a book— always inconsequential trivialities disconnected and immediately forgotten.

Sometimes Green's gaze drifted down to his right leg, swathed in plaster of Paris with a rubber tread fitted to the foot. It never seemed to belong. Why was it attached to his body? Once the thought occurred to him: *am I here because of that?*

Then, quite suddenly: *no!* A tiny insight at last, but one with large consequences.

A change was observed in Green—not that too much could be expected, not so soon, not *this* time! But his personality appeared to be undergoing a slow and laborious repair. Nobody expected a miracle, for Green was, at most, a partially rebuilt house with, so to speak, a new wall or two, a mended roof, a repainted door—but still piles of debris hidden inside.

The staff found Green unpredictable. Sometimes voluble, sometimes moody and morose. He was cocky and rebellious; acquiescent and meek. He would take his medication without complaint, or perhaps he would not. He might get up at a reasonable hour or stay in bed until two orderlies had to drag him out to keep an appointment with a therapist.

Sometimes they preferred Green as he had been!

Bad days, when Green thumped about, broken leg and all, shouting derisive abuse. Better days when he'd lie quietly smoking endless home-rolled cigarettes, listening to the portable radio or shuffling listlessly through magazines; starting to read an article but never getting to the end; or reaching the last sentence of a paragraph with no recollection of the first.

There were many attempts, but nobody, as yet, had ever succeeded in coaxing Green out—save (and then with often violent protests) for his necessary treatments and interviews in one of the rooms along the white corridor.

Green was clearly confused as to identities. He rarely remembered a name, grasped any distinction between orderly, nurse or doctor. Often it was as if everyone who opened the door, white coated or not, was an intruder, an enemy. According to his current state of mind he would shrink back, or shout an epithet, or merely glare in suspicion and mutter insults.

Green was developing a colourful repertoire of invective and scathing abuse which endeared him to nobody. Sick or not, the staff agreed Green was a pain in the neck—and probably always had been.

The broad window was double-glazed and high up the building. It had green curtains on rings. There was a very wide and distant view, rural, with copses and undulating fields where cattle grazed and a partially tree-hidden, low-built farmhouse too far off for much in the way of human activity to be observed.

A tractor sometimes emerged from the shadow and crawled through a gate into a winding lane. At a greater distance still stood a cluster of pottery chimneys oozing white vapour. It was a varied spring scene, frequently bathed in soft sunshine, until clouds gathered and threw thin shadows across the fields. On occasion a fresh wind bent the trees and there were bouts of streaking rain.

Closest of all, for Green, forever shimmering in a haze, was the stretch of motorway. At two points elegant white concrete bridges bestraddled it. The road fascinated Green and, in certain moods, he felt himself caught as if in a time warp. A memory would stir, then be at once dissolved—*something past, or something future?*

The road would gleam brighter, as bright as a vision, contemptuously bisecting a dull deadland on each side of it. There was all the swift and throbbing procession of fast inter-city traffic and the diesel-thrust of transcontinental trucks.

The scene made Green uneasy, so that he'd shift his focus to more natural and remote objects: a flight of starlings perched like black dots on spangled wires, or sheep in the distant meadow.

Apart from the radio and magazines, the room contained little to amuse Green. Was this, he wondered, with a flash of new cunning, a trick with which to flush him out? Of his own property they'd left only a tartan-patterned case. It stood in the whitewood wardrobe, on the floor under the hospital dressing gown. At some point Green, floundering towards yet another oasis in his darkened memory, vaguely recognized it as his own. It felt empty and unimportant: Green did not bother to open it.

There was a second bed in the room, against the opposite wall by the wardrobe. No occupant...except that sometimes in the night Green woke and thought he heard the sound of breathing. They'd planted a night orderly in here, then? To make sure that he didn't masturbate—say more than once a week?

Some such ribald thought, humourless and without significance, would flutter through his head—before, not bothering to switch on his light, he would fall asleep and forget.

The bathroom and toilet were in a separate cubicle between the door of his room and a second one which they kept locked, opening into the corridor.

But he had the luxury of a tiny wash basin, above which was a small white cabinet, with mirror. The cabinet contained toilet requisites in sparse supply. No razor, no scissors: just a pair of nail clippers, some toothpaste and a brush.

Green found his image in the mirror disturbing and he would gaze at it with baffled intensity—as if the face shining there was the photograph of a stranger, but a stranger offering some unfathomable menace.

The eyes were brown, set rather narrow over a pointed nose. The face was brown bearded, not yet lush. Above the unsmiling mouth curved a promising moustache, in need of more elegant trimming, like the almost hippie length brown and slightly frizzled hair.

Green came to dislike the face so much that, once in front of the cabinet, he would swing the little door far back on its hinges and attend to his ablutions without assistance from the image in the glass.

2

Dr Simpson, senior psychiatrist, was a slight, spruce man with unobtrusively probing blue eyes and a voice that would give comfort to a mourner at a graveside.

'Hello, David.' Sometimes he hesitated on the name as if he'd momentarily forgotten it. 'How does the leg feel?'

'Okay, ta.' They'd removed Green's plaster a few days ago and, instead of hobbling along to the doctor's office on crutches, he'd arrived by stick.

'Fine. Now you'll be able to get out a little.'

'Where?'

'The grounds are quite pleasant. There's a cricket match on tomorrow.'

Not too much enthusiasm from Green—or perhaps his concentration had lapsed again. Dr Simpson was using a simple technique: a concealed stop watch with which to measure Green's increasing ability to sustain a conversation. Question—answer. Comment—retort. The bizarre break-aways, the occasional monologues, even the silences, were faithfully recorded on an equally invisible tape machine in the half open drawer beside him.

'How are you sleeping these days, David?' asked Dr Simpson, making a fresh start.

'Not bad. Pills upset my stomach.'

'They shouldn't...I'm told you sometimes refuse to take them.'

'Well, they can always squat on my chest and squeeze my nose, can't they?'

'I'd rather you co-operated, David. Especially with the capsules. Not only are they extremely expensive but they form a vital part of your treatment.'

'For a broken leg?' scoffed Green. Then: 'What exactly's supposed to be wrong with me?'

The first time Green had asked. Dr Simpson said, carefully, 'Nothing we can't handle, David—in time.'

Green said, 'I don't want to go out and mix with a lot of nut cases. Most of the staff are barmy, too! How long are you keeping me?'

'Not keeping you, David. This isn't a prison.'

'Go on?' said Green, still on track. 'But it's a loony bin, right?'

'Not at all,' temporized Dr Simpson. 'As a matter of fact this is a general hospital, two miles or so out of town. We have a medical wing, a casualty department—even a maternity unit.' Too evasive, of course. He began to add, hoping Green wouldn't overreact, 'I do, admittedly, run a little show of my own under the same roof, but....'

Green sneered. 'Maternity unit! Don't tell me. I'm pregnant! So that accounts for the screams in the night.'

'Screams?'

'Babies...I'd got round to thinking you were torturing political prisoners.'

Dr Simpson smiled and relaxed—a little too soon. He caught Green's sudden movement of gaze, the run

11

of his fingers through the flimsy beard which invariably heralded a mind-shift. At least, for the time being, there would be no more of Green's so-called jokes.

'The motorway keeps me awake.'

'Ah, yes, the motorway.'

'Bloody diesels thumping by all night. Why the hell did they build it close to a hospital?' No break, straight on: 'I remember it all, now, clear as daylight. You asked me to say what I remembered, and when. I've been holding out on you.'

'Have you, David?'

'Well, it was depression, wasn't it? What made me try it, like. Plenty of people get depression, they want to stop the world and get off. Gas themselves, chuck themselves into rivers, take an overdose. That's how it was with me, wasn't it? I mean, I'd just fluffed it at art school. Didn't even make the first year so they chucked me out.'

There was a closed file on Dr Simpson's desk— somebody else's. Green nodded at it and went on. 'You must have all this on my record.'

'Carry on, David.'

'It was as if I could see my own death that morning. It was raining like hell. I remember thinking, road'll be slippery. I thought of the driver of the truck—I'd worked out it ought to be a big truck because it was less likely anybody else would get hurt.

'He was out there somewhere on the road, heading my way, only he wouldn't know, would he? I stuffed half a bottle of whisky in my tunic, drank the lot before taking off. On the way I felt pretty high—crazy, you know? I was getting a kick out of knowing that pretty soon I'd be just a heap of broken bones. I even laughed

12

at the thought of my own blood all over the road.

'There was this stretch of double carriage way. I'd picked it beforehand, noticing there were no safety barriers. I revved up to seventy, maybe eighty, then I saw this truck coming and I thought, I'm all yours, baby! Don't worry, mate, you won't feel a thing.

'Hell, he must have had reactions of a bloody sparrow. I couldn't have been more than a few yards away when he saw me coming across and swerved. Instead of hitting him square on, all I did was glance his side then went into a spin and landed up on the central reservation.

'Police car was on my tail by then. I was lying there, leg busted, and there was this copper haring towards me reaching for his notebook. For a minute I thought he was going to book me for speeding!'

Green had been pouring all this out, talking faster and faster until sweat glistened on his forehead. Now he seemed exhausted, eyes vaguely fixed on the window.

He said, at last, looking back at Dr Simpson, 'Must have got concussion, too, right? Helmet came loose, say. That's how I lost my memory. How am I doing?'

Dr Simpson tapped gently with his ball pen. 'Very well, David.'

Green nodded with the sudden little-boy's solemnity which occasionally peeped through the brashness. He said, 'So I failed again, didn't I? I bet the bike made a better job of itself. Suzuki, wasn't it? And a write-off. Japs grinning all over their faces, sticking up two fingers, or whatever they do in Tokyo, having their own back for Hiroshima!'

Dr Simpson gave Green a long, hard look. 'Tell me,

13

David, how do you feel now?'

'Feel...what?'

'You want to live, don't you?'

The familiar grin not reflected in the brown eyes. 'Don't fancy dying much—not again.'

'Again?'

'Well, there're these lousy dreams, aren't there? The one about the coffin's worst.'

'A coffin?'

'There's this coffin....'

'Tell me about it, David....'

'There's a name on it.'

'*What* name, David?'

'How the hell do I know? Anyway, I'm not sure it's always a coffin. Sometimes it's a grave....'

Dr Simpson's temporary assistant, two years or so out of medical school, found the senior psychiatrist's habit of using him as a sounding board instructive as well as flattering.

He handed back the reports and tapes he had borrowed and said, 'Rum character.'

'Very.'

'This motorway business....'

'Yes, his hallucinations are most elaborate. Probably in colour too!'

'This claim that he's recovering his memory....'

'Dreams,' said Dr Simpson. 'Almost entirely dreams. To put it technically....'

He did so. His assistant practically clung to his seat, then said, 'At least we're doing no worse than anybody else.'

'I hope not. These new drugs can be damned tricky

14

and the young blighter appears to flush half of them down the toilet! Let me see....' He leafed through a file. 'At Dukesbury, they thought they were making progress with a truth drug.'

'I thought they only cropped up in old American movies.'

'At Glanbury Park,' went on Dr Simpson, 'their approach was hypnosis. As you know, I'm not a devotee—just haven't got the knack.'

'Me neither! Tried it once, with a swinging watch. Nearly cracked the patient's nose.'

'We shall have to get him out of that room, somehow. Open ward, group therapy, the usual sort of thing. An entirely new programme, in fact.'

The young doctor said, cynically, 'Cups of tea every hour on the hour? Ludo? Cards? Fag swapping?'

Dr Simpson frowned in partial disapproval—but only partial. He'd had a busy day and felt a little institutional humour was permissible. 'There's the Scandinavian thing...what's the jargon? Hate therapy? The poor little devil would probably jump at it. Make his life a worse hell that it already is, then plant a meat knife in his bed and let him come at us with it. Any volunteers?'

The assistant said, seriously, 'If you'd like me to see more of Green....'

'I wish you would. In his own habitat, as it were. A new face might make a difference. I've had staff in here threatening to resign in the last week.'

'Just thinking aloud...but can't we just *tell* him the truth?'

'No! I don't wish to dabble in philosophy, but truth works better when it comes from within. Oh, and by the

15

way...don't address him as *Green*. He prefers, I think, to be called *David.*'

3

There was a fair degree of clinical progress, in Dr Simpson's view. Green holding on longer and longer to conversational sequences, laughing, jeering, scowling—mostly in the right places. Increasingly quick on the uptake, less inclined to withdraw into a shell, and irritatingly loquacious.

But his past life evidently remained, to all intents and purposes, buried in a shroud. There had been that one, extraordinarily vivid and detailed account of the motor-bike crash and the events leading up to it but, afterwards, no further references. Green, moreover, had related the story in the flat, half uninterested manner one might adopt in toying with speculations about a state of existence before birth. And Dr Simpson remained convinced: to *tell* Green, even to feed him clues would, at best, have little more effect than a mother confiding in her child how it had been when he'd first quickened in her womb.

So for Green, increasingly abandoned to solitude by reluctant orderlies, his daily thoughts and impressions arrived as haphazardly as his meals. He drank the long light through the window, swallowed the minutes, chewed at the hours.

It was around midday by the little wall clock when

the familiar key clicked in the outer door and somebody knocked. Actually knocked before bursting in!

No lunch. No white coat. The stranger wore casuals—jeans, a scruffy parka hanging loosely over a polo-neck sweater. He was a young man bearing a superficial, same-generation resemblance to Green—beard style, moustache, hair (though closer cut).

He smiled at Green. 'Have I got the right room? You *are* David? New around here. Spend most of my time buzzing about like a lost bee in a bottle. Name's Steve.'

Nothing so pompous as a handshake. And Green didn't shift his hands, linked behind his head on the propped pillow. 'How did you get hold of the key?'

'Pardon?'

'To my room. You a patient?'

'Does it show? Actually, I work here—sort of. I'm supposed to be learning the ropes, getting to know people. Mind if I squat?' He helped himself to the small armchair Green never used. 'Wondered if there was anything you needed.'

'Yes, my lunch. Meals are getting later and later. Bleeders will finish up pushing the muck under the door. They think I'm the Count of Monte Cristo.'

Steve glanced at the crack. 'They'll have to make it pancakes!'

'I shan't notice the difference.'

A bit more of this sort of chat, Green not asking questions, not asking who and what Steve was, exactly. Steve would have told him, if necessary. Meanwhile he felt easier with his partial anonymity. Just another bod around the place Green thought? Steve was glad he hadn't brought his stethoscope!

18

He was propped up on one elbow, now, eyes focused at an awkward angle along the length of the bed on Steve's face. Very intent. Steve was a long time getting the message.

He said, 'I gather you're an art student.'

'Was,' said Green.

'Before your accident?'

'It wasn't an accident.' Gaze still locked on Steve. A twist of the mouth. '*You* should know that.'

'Should I?'

Green's antipathy was unnerving. Steve shook himself clear of the eyes by getting up, removing his jacket—the room was over heated—and hanging it on the chair.

Green had lain back by then, staring at the ceiling, thank heavens! Some time before he drawled, 'Don't tell me you haven't read my dossier? Every other bugger in this stinking place has. They're handed out free copies to take to the bog with them!'

'I was only thinking,' said Steve, evasively. 'There's an art room downstairs. You haven't seen it? Pretty well equipped, not much used so far as I can see....'

'Stuff it,' said Green.

'Tell you what, then. I'll fetch some things up here. Tomorrow, say? Easel, paper, paints...as a matter of fact I like dabbling a bit myself. Not in your class, of course—perhaps you can give me some tips.' He added, more or less because Green hadn't immediately flung a new obscenity in his face, 'I'll have a bit of time on my hands for the next couple of weeks. After that I'm off on a course—in London.'

Green's eyes leapt back at once, suddenly shining. The window light—or images projected through chinks in his brain?

Steve tingled—or was it just a touch of the horrors? He'd probed with too little knowledge. He'd deliberately tantalized—and that against orders. Too soon, with too much naïvety (this chap might still be off his nut, but he was bright) Steve had tried to winkle out his mislaid soul with a pick axe. Not very clever, Doctor! Who do you think you are—Sigmund Freud?

The rest, though, had been a pure coincidence. How was Steve to have known?

There was no photograph of Green on file.

'No,' said Dr Simpson, tapping his pen. 'Well, yes...there may be no harm in trying out the paints thing. Don't be surprised if he chucks the lot in your face!'

'For the rest,' said Steve, 'you think I should skip psychiatry and go for obstetrics?'

'I merely think that too much theory and we shall be on a hiding to nothing.' Dr Simpson peered at his assistant's face. 'There isn't *that* close a resemblance, you know.'

'But *he* thinks so...sir,' argued Steve, hoping that a touch of deference might help him push his foot a little farther through the slightly open door. 'And I believe I was subconsciously aware of a likeness too. That may be why...well, I've admitted to passing the ball a shade too soon. But I'm certain he began to establish some kind of identification, a personality transference ...what exactly do they call it?'

'I've no idea!' said Dr Simpson, drily. 'I *am* of the opinion that they teach too much psychology at medical school these days—and badly, at that. Or do I mean rugger?'

'But it's all right if I press on?'

'Yes. No! That is, observation and dabbling in paint, yes. Starting up your own private miracle clinic, no. And I'd appreciate a detailed report after every session.'

'Of course.' Steve wasn't being put off by a threat of extra paperwork. 'It'll only be for a couple of weeks.'

'That's partly what worries me. I've had some patients for twenty years and they still think I'm a reincarnation of Ghengiz Khan.'

Steve felt depressed. 'Why do you do it? Why do I still think *I* want to do it? There must be other areas of medical practice in which one feels...well, more effective.'

Dr Simpson sighed, but no more or less cheerfully than usual. 'I don't know, Steve. Thoreau.' And he quoted: '"The mass of men lead lives of quiet desperation." However, should you put our David back on the road before trotting off to your course in the great city, I'll personally see that you are nominated for a Nobel Prize.'

Green, who only sometimes remembered his dreams, would nevertheless be aware, on waking, that they had coursed through his sleeping mind—like random subterranean waters leaving ridges of silt on which were footprints, or the scratched images of faces.

One face tonight, like his own but not his own: yet not entirely another's. His cortex worried over the enigma, nagged at it, strained over its mystery—then he sweated awake.

He'd forgotten to draw the curtains. Through the

21

window the moon hung full, leaping as bright as a low star through wisps of flying cloud.

The drone of traffic from the motorway throbbed in his ears—then the scream. The scream was born out of the diesel thunder, was at first part of it; it had the metallic reasonance of tortured steel. Then, still at full pitch, it soared lark-like, but wilder and more frantic than any bird. The scream diminished into the sky.

Silence at last, even the road was silent. Green could never reach his light without acrobatics. He groped in the dark. *'You rotten little sod,'* he said aloud. *'Have you hidden my syringe again?'*

Then he found the single sleeping pill on the floor beside his bed—that and the half spilt mug of tepid water.

4

It wasn't working, Steve decided—whatever he was supposed to be trying to achieve. Nothing in particular, he admitted. To begin with he had simply been fascinated by Green's file—who wouldn't be? The other factors—the partial resemblance between them and Green's obvious response—were unexpected extras. The sceptical but tolerant Dr Simpson had reluctantly given Steve his head and, no doubt, expected him to crawl back with egg on his face.

Egg, but at least no scattered paint. Nothing so violent or traumatic from Green. He simply remained propped on his pillow, rolling his cigarettes and occasionally looking on, with no apparent interest, as Steve self-consciously erected the easel, prepared palette and brushes and fetched water from the wash basin.

'Want to show me what you can do?'

Green said, 'You lumped the gear up, chum. You Cezanne, me Jane.'

Witty stuff today!

Steve chatted about this and that as he daubed on the paper. He kept within his limitations: a colourful, complex and utterly spurious abstract, all whorls and wiggles and eyes popping at the ends of hideous and fortuitous stalks.

'How's that?'

'Lousy.' The gaze was upon Steve rather than on the painting. Then: 'When's it you're going down to the smoke?'

'Pardon? Oh, the course. End of next week.'

Green asked, 'Where?'

'Where what?'

'Where in London?'

Green had remembered about *that?*

'Place called Tooting. A hospital there....'

Session two, next day, and shorter. Somebody, probably Green, had pushed the easel into a corner, folded with the painting smeared and flattened against the wall. No masterpiece discernible from Green, no comment, same slouch on the bed.

Bits of conversation for ten minutes, Steve clipping on a fresh sheet of paper to the easel—he felt even less convinced, this time, of any possible result.

Green let him half finish before he said, 'Too much blue.'

'You think so?'

'I know so. Balance is all to hell, too. Why do you bother?'

'I enjoy it.'

'What sort of answer is that? Reckon you'll ever make a living at it?'

'Of course not....'

Green said, 'Come off it, kid. You know you think you're a bloody little Rembrandt. When you buzz off to London, or wherever, do me a favour and cart all that mush away with you. Stick it on somebody else's wall and let *them* vomit.'

Steve wished he'd risked a mini cassette recorder. He'd remember the words for the purposes of his report, so called, but there would be no reliable means of conveying tones and cadences. Nor the quiet, cruel savagery of the drawn out vowels and spitting consonants.

Steve couldn't withstand the stare much longer. He began packing up the equipment—end of experiment. He sent for an orderly to take it back to the art room. Green made no comment.

Yes, Steve decided—obstetrics. Or possibly paediatrics. Give him babies wetting on his lap every time!

A new orderly, Green supposed. And he hadn't brought him his tea. The outer door had clicked, then the brass handle inside turned slowly, as if with a purposeful stealth, and the bulky figure stood there, eyes straight on Green.

He wore a stained white coat, a couple of sizes too small so that a button had burst loose from the barrel chest. No, not just an orderly, Green thought. Somebody higher up, the way he swaggered in, heeled the door shut, stood with his back to the window, blew into a filthy handkerchief then lit a cigarette using a curious tube-shaped lighter with a softly glowing wick. He had dark jowls, piggy eyes, a mouthful of broken brown teeth. 'You Green?'

'Yeah.'

'Call me sir—and stand up.'

'I've got a bad leg.'

'I know about your leg, Green. There's a lot I know about you. All right, stay there on your arse but talk civil—and only when I tell you to. Savvy? They've sent me along to straighten you out. You'll be seeing a lot of me from now on. Name's Hogg—*Mister* Hogg. Who am I?'

'Mister Hogg,' said Green, mesmerized.

The man waddled away from the window, so close that as he loomed over Green hot ash dropped from his cigarette on to the pillow.

Green was smoking. Hogg curled his lips. 'Who said you could have matches?'

'Why shouldn't I have matches?'

' "Why shouldn't I have matches, please, Mr Hogg." I'll tell you why you shouldn't have matches, Greeno. Because you're a nasty little squirt who tried to do away with himself, that's why.' Hogg slipped the box into the pocket of his dirty coat. For a second or two his hovering face smelt of tobacco and sweat. 'I'll be back, Greeno, I'll be back. *Mister* Hogg—got it? Shifting you to maximum security block where I'm the bloke with the big stick, not Dr Simpson. Along with all the other killers.'

A night of wilder dreams still for Green. Hazily, next morning he thought he'd dreamt up Hogg, too. Then he couldn't find his matches.

The knob turned early. The same stealth, the hideous remembered figure strutting to the brightening window where it indulged in a masquerade of wordless threat—a cough, a sneeze into a handkerchief thick with mucus, the fresh cigarette.

Then, as if precisely continuing the monologue of yesterday, Hogg said, 'You're worse than a killer, Greeno. In my book, suicide is the big one, the crime nobody gets away with.' A monstrous shrug, a play with Green's matches, rattling the box, tossing it in his hand. 'Still, that's only half of it, Greeno. Know what? If I had it my way I'd burn down places like this. Ashes to ashes, like, and all of us along with it. You reckon I enjoy this job? I get up in the morning and it's just another lousy day. I have a pee, I shave, and I think: what's the bad news this time? Who gets the chopper? Could be anybody, Greeno. Could even be you.'

He drifted nearer—and nearer. 'Do you know what used to happen to suicides? In the Middle Ages, in some countries, the body was not allowed to be brought through a door. They lowered it through a window on pulleys, then burned the window frame. How about that, eh? The stoics…them blokes treated 'em exactly as they did their garbage. In England they was treated like murderers and hung from a gibbet, then buried at the cross roads with a stake through their heart. Scares you, does it, Greeno? You want to live after all? Better put in your application to the Home Office quick, then, before we take your plug out—just to save you the trouble. Happens most nights, Greeno. In the dead hours, somebody gets his. Don't you never hear their groans?'

'Incredible!' said Dr Simpson. 'Did you tell him?'

'I tried. He didn't take it in, though. He's still very confused about people, isn't he? Who's real and who isn't.'

'But he's frightened?'

'Shaking like a jelly.'

'That's new!'

'Could help to concentrate his mind—or what's left

of it.'

'I'd better see him myself. And Hogg. We really shall have to do something about Hogg. I don't know what the staff are about—far too lax, despite my instructions. Letting him strut about in that damned coat. And I never do find out how he gets hold of those keys.'

'Probably wins them at cards!'

'The other week I actually found him in here, leafing through the confidential files.'

'Gracious!'

'There's something else on your mind.'

'Sorry...not sure how to tell you.'

'You'd better try.'

'It's my loss—except for the keys.'

'What is?'

'Hogg's cleaned me out. I'd hung my jacket in David's room while I was trying to calm him down. Then, as I said, Hogg pitched up again. I thought it best to let him hang about for a bit, hoping that in my presence David would realize he was only another patient. The wretched creature showed no sign of leaving, though. I tried to shove him through the door, but I didn't cut much ice....'

'On a good day,' sighed Dr Simpson, 'Hogg eats members of the Regional Committee. Go on.'

'Hogg must have lifted everything while my back was turned. Nearly a hundred quid in the wallet—and my keys.'

'Surely you've checked?'

'Of course. Ran Hogg down in the main ward. The blighter had been too quick for me. Nothing on him—except a few pounds he'd probably won off the charge

28

nurse at poker. The first lot of keys, of course...and a box of matches he'd taken from David.'

'Matches! He's *never* allowed within a mile of matches. The brute was a top grade arsonist among other things! You had everything turned over? Mattresses and so forth?'

'Yes, the lot. The staff know most of his tricks. They're as baffled as I am.'

Dr Simpson's face was slowly turning grey, a phenomenon not altogether to be explained by the deepening light of early evening. 'Tell me, Steve, when you set off in pursuit of Hogg, who locked David's room?'

'I yelled at an orderly.'

'Which one?'

'Young Indian chap.'

'That'll be Shinti. Recent immigrant—knows a dozen words of English. He may not have understood. Steve, when you tried to push friend Hogg out of the door, your jacket was still on David's chair?'

A sunset blush from Steve. 'I say, I hope I haven't been *that* stupid.'

'So do I!' said Dr Simpson, standing up abruptly. 'A headless chicken could get a long way on a hundred pounds.'

5

As soon as Steve had gone in pursuit of Hogg, the
pinions of Green's mind slipped, without fuss, into a
different gear. Hyperdrive, almost—a short thrust out
of apathetic chaos.

He retrieved the wallet from beneath his pillow,
together with the small bunch of keys on their ring.
He'd noticed that both doors into the corridor were
wide open, but his fugitive cunning told him there
might be others.

He took the wad of money from the wallet, flung the
wallet itself on to his bed and stuffed the notes into a
back pocket.

There were no extra clothes, nothing of importance.
Fishing his tartan case out of the wardrobe was an
afterthought. It belonged to him. It was right that he
should take it.

Green met no challenge in the corridor. Somebody
was cleaning the toilet and its flush damped the passing
footsteps. A flight of stone stairs, then another, then a
third. A glass panelled door overlooking a vegetable
plot required a key. Unhurriedly, Green found the
correct one, left the door unlocked and followed a
rectangular gravel path. He flung the keys into the
cabbages.

No attendant stopped him at the main gate. Having no idea, nor even any immediate concern, which direction to take Green limped to a road devoid of traffic, leading down, down towards the spires and roofs of the city. Someone might have caught up with him in time, except that he found a footpath, hidden by trees and shrubs in lush full leaf, following a stream on and on down to the River Trent. Nearing the town, Green sat on the wall of a bridge, looking at swans. His leg ached.

He felt no sense of triumph. He was puzzled by what he had done. There were no words, yet in a confused way his brain was asking: *am I following, or being followed?*

The print-out instructions of a once ordinary, everyday life steered him with the sureness of a treadmill to the station.

There were terraced cottages on each side of him, the square, a clock tower. Another short street led up an access path to the station.

The shadow was there—sometimes before him and sometimes after. Green quickened his limping stride.

At the booking office he bought a single ticket for Euston, Intercity. He might have had more than an hour to wait but in less than ten minutes the train glided into the platform.

Green chose a smokers' compartment, chucking his almost empty tartan case carelessly on to the rack above. He sat down and watched through the filmy window. The pottery kilns oozed smoke and steam. He carefully took out his tin of tobacco and rolled himself a cigarette—an orderly had brought him fresh matches.

Green waited without impatience for the journey to start. Thoughts darted about in his head, stuttering like a disorientated computer. The ghosts of his dreams reappeared like actors on an overcrowded stage, none with true identities, all fluffing their lines, but each insistent upon being heard.

The train left the station. Time passed. The sky was darkening, now, lending a mirror's reflectiveness to the window—and there was a face.

A face much like Green's but, again, another's. A face which he never wanted to see—not any more—yet he would be destroyed were he denied it! Green tried to pass his tobacco tin to the face. The tin clattered against the glass, spilling its contents on the seat.

'All right, kid. Buy your own fags.'

Green carefully picked up the shreds of tobacco, retrieved the cigarette papers, stuffed everything back into the tin, turned instinctively with his back to the window.

Once he took out the roll of notes. The one-way ticket had diminished it but little. Ninety-one pounds! He counted it twice. He felt briefly elated. He murmured aloud, aware of a stab of guilt: *'Well, you asked for it. Fair shares, remember? I'm almost expected to share your bloody toothbrush!'*

Green wasn't guilty about a young doctor called Steve: in no real sense did either Steve or the hospital exist any more.

After this Green slept, waking only once when the inspector swayed by to clip his ticket. As the train slid into Euston he woke again, heart racing, limbs cold.

He staggered towards the door, grasping at the rails as if the train was still moving at top speed. He stepped down on to a windy platform, then remembered that he'd forgotten his tartan case. He lurched back to retrieve it. He was shivering convulsively, teeth chattering. An early summer's night in London! He zipped up his parka and made for the lights beyond the barrier.

Not a station he knew, not a city he remembered. Beyond the glass walls fine rain hissed across a row of bright buses. Green stared at them, wondering whether to tag on to the queue of mushroomed umbrellas. He soon lost track of why he had considered this.

He stood outside the station, clutching his case like a baffled tourist from some remote country not even knowing the language. Then he moved off into the rain. He picked out the glow of a pub sign across the lines of traffic. He found a crossing and waited obediently till the little green man showed. Then, still shivering, he bent his head into the rain and followed a different line of umbrellas.

He never noticed the name of the pub, a large, sprawling, seedy place with several bars. Smoke and voices and juke-box music oozed through window lights.

Green pushed open the door. The lounge bar was plusher than one might have expected. Coloured bulbs hung over a long counter, red leather chairs and round glass-topped tables nestled in dim corners beneath soft wall lamps.

Green fished a fiver out of his jeans and ordered a double rum. The sea-shanty picture on the bottle had beguiled him. And a coke. Green tried to pour coke

33

into the rum, spilling a lot on the bar.

He stayed there for several minutes, sipping at his drink, mind struggling to cohere. Phrases popped up, starkly brilliant and commanding the darkness like neon lights:

THEY HAVEN'T BROUGHT MY BLOODY CAPSULES. ONE REALITY IS AS GOOD AS ANOTHER. HE NEVER CARED WHAT HAPPENED TO ME. WAIT TILL HE KNOWS—HE'LL BE SORRY.

There was nobody close in the dim corner. Nobody concerned with Green, nobody finding him worth a second glance.

A pretty brunette sat seductively six feet away, hair dripping over her face, with a predatory-eyed companion clutching her waist. Just two more vagrant parasites using the pub as host.

Green took another swig at his drink. His hands steadied perceptibly. He was aware of a sort of freedom—as if his soul had been handed back.

Another flash: YOU'RE ON YOUR OWN NOW, BROTHER. MAKE YOUR OWN DECISIONS—thought accompanied by the fleeting glimpse of the face in the glass-topped table.

'*Time you made some decisions of your own, kid. And lay off the hard stuff.*'

'*You can talk! If it's your filthy syringe you're looking for...and I have made decisions. I'm brassed off with being your shadow.*'

A new shadow fell across the table, a middle-aged man bearing a remembered shabbiness—ill-fitting suit wet from the rain, stained striped shirt, with a studded collar and string tie askew. The stubble chin lent the sallow face the expression of a morgue attendant, forgetting yesterday's shaving—or living.

'Anybody's seat?'

'No.'

'Raining cats and dogs out there.'

The whisky fumes hit Green like poison gas. The man sucked at his glass. Green fumbled for his tobacco tin but the rum had got into his fingers. The man was watching.

He took out a pouch of his own and spilt it across the table. 'Help yourself.'

'Forget it!'

'Better to stick to your own poison, like?' The hunger for companionship made the eyes inquisitive. 'Just off a train?'

'Yeah.'

'Picked up your accent. Birmingham way?'

Green didn't answer.

'Never been to Birmingham.' The man struck a red-tipped match for Green, watching the groping fingers. He emptied his glass. 'Something wrong with my face?'

'Sorry?'

'You're getting an eyeful of it!'

'We never know how to take you.'

'Come again?'

'You wouldn't be on the scrounge, just by way of a change, like?'

The man froze, still clutching his empty glass. He got the words out, slurred but articulate with indignation. 'What are you drinking there, son? Nitro-bloody-glycerine? I'd take the train back where you came from if I was you. At your age an' all.'

It was some moments before Green even noticed the

empty chair. There was the smouldering stub of a fag in the ashtray, smoking in a little grave of ashes.

The floor tilted, the rafters of the ceiling bent.

Green lurched from the table. He forgot his case, remembered to go back and fetch it, bumped into things on his way out.

Out into the windy-wet night.

6

The rain eased a little but a damp wind still gusted along the main street.

Green limped into it, swaying precariously at first. The pavement was a narrow ledge with a chasm on each side. He had no idea how far he walked, nor that he was travelling roughly in squares: when he turned a corner, it was always to the right.

He knew where he was, London. Westminster Abbey, Buckingham Palace, Trafalgar Square. These were names and symbols, leap-frogging through his whistling brain with no precise relevance but reassuring him that he had arrived somewhere—somewhere he had long wanted to be.

In due course he steadied again: the pavement broadened, he no longer reeled from side to side clutching at railings and posts.

He was in a quiet square. There were stars in the sky and a waning moon. There was a little park to his left, full of silver trees. He saw everything in sharply etched detail—lighted bell pushes in doorways up flights of steps, a single milk bottle stranded below, a missing railing in the park fence.

Green suddenly wanted to sleep. His thoughts were becoming better connected, like a reunion of scattered bones. He addressed himself, sometimes aloud, and there was no eavesdropper, no clinical observer, to attempt a mapping out of his thoughts.

Self mockery, without bitterness; blasphemy expressing no rejection of a god; obscenity with no present sex drive.

This was London, wasn't it? And you could sleep anywhere. Under a railway arch, on a park seat, or a bench on the embankment. (Where the hell was the embankment?)

The Y.M.C.A., if he could find one. The Warden sniffing his breath, a cup of cocoa, a plain narrow bed in a dormitory? Sod that!

Pick up a tart? There would be cards in shop windows advertising massage parlours—so maybe he'd wind up having his back rubbed by a thick fingered Greek ex-wrestler. He'd pay twenty quid for the privilege and get chucked out on the street.

All this was a part of Green, the *old* Green, but it didn't last.

The spectres returned, demanding admittance, dragging in a corpse as lively as a dancing skeleton.

That damned face eyed Green out of a shop window...and his mood plunged at once. There were times when Green could master simple optical realities, but there were others when the image in glass was neither ghost nor projection, but something malevolent which would never let him go, never set him free....

Now it set off in pursuit, stepping out of the window and dogging his steps—Green could hear its footfall on the pavement after him.

But it kept its distance, watching, biding its time,

breathing out of the dark like a mugger poised to make a kill.

Green knew it was late, time to get off the street. He found a hotel with a broken light over the porch. They'd left a shifty-eyed youth on duty at the reception desk, who yawned in bored surprise as Green approached. He pushed his magazine away and consulted a list. 'Twelve quid, B. and B. That do you, mate?'

He reached for a key and slid it across the counter. 'Room twenty-two, fourth floor. Lift's not working. Reckon you can find it?'

'Sure.'

'Don't pee in the basin, mate. There's a bog on the landing below. Breakfast eight sharp, if you want it. You pay then.' A quickening of curiosity. 'You look bushed. Been on the razzle?'

'Yeah.'

'Better sign the register.'

Green's shaky entry read, *D. Green—Birmingham*.

Green picked up his case and made it up the stairs. At the top he was breathless and dizzy. He had a problem focusing on the numbers of the rooms—there were half a dozen on this floor. Frayed carpet, very dim lights. A woman giggled through one of the doors.

Green found number twenty-two, got the key into the lock, went in, relocked the door behind him, groped for a light switch.

The shade was of broken plastic and had a forty watt light bulb. Single bed with a faded cover, cracked wash basin with two taps, one of them dripping. A mirrored cabinet over the top reminded him of somewhere. The papered ceiling had a dip in the middle and cobwebs over the light.

The curtain was half closed over a pair of glass doors. Green tried the handle and the door opened on to the iron landing of a fire escape. He shut the door, redrew the curtains, sat on the bed.

He was feeling sick. He peeled off his parka, kicked off his shoes, slung the tartan case into a corner.

The room span. He got up and crashed across to the wash basin. The smoky little mirror had a crack from top to bottom, distorting it so that it gave back a double image.

Green muttered, 'For Chrissake, not *two* of the bastards!'

He flung back the cabinet door and leaned over the basin, nose bent inside. He was violently sick into the basin, propping a hand upon each tap and twisting both on. He stooped there, panting until it was over, then urinated and turned the taps off.

Green was too exhausted to undress. He pulled the cover aside and flung himself on to the single pillow. The whine in his head rose to a crescendo and whirled him into oblivion....

The dream had no setting, no place, no room. There was simply a shift of shapes, and their father's face, breath heavy with whisky, held there—somewhere—as in a spotlight.

The badly fitting suit, the striped shirt, no tie, hat on his knees, a straggling disarray of hair over his ears.

'Had a hell of a job finding where you was. You could have looked me up. Listen, it wasn't my fault, was it? I thought they'd have let you know. What the hell was he doing down there, on his own? Never

40

used to let him out of your sight!

'Still, you weren't kids no more, was you? Got anything to drink? I meant to bring something with me, just to keep out the cold, like. Don't worry, I'm not on the scrounge. Matter of fact, I've been having a bit of luck with the dogs lately, plus a bit of wheeling and dealing....'

Their old man got out his tobacco tin, rolled himself a fag, lit it, pushed the tin across, spat tobacco.

'He went clean off the rails, you know? What the hell was he supposed to be trying to prove? They reckoned he didn't suffer—no pain or nothing. Bike was a write-off, but I hear there's some insurance due....

'Only me at the crematorium, apart from a few dogsbodies. Nice funeral, as these things go. Sunny morning, and all. I bought a wreath—from the two of us. They asked me what hymn they should play. I couldn't think of anything except "Abide with me"....'

The half burnt cigarette slipped out of his fingers and he bent down to pick it up. He drew on it and sneezed. He carefully wiped the hairs of his nose.

'Had a little tree planted for him—a rose tree. Gardens of Remembrance, shady place near a stone wall. And there's this inscription, a quote from the Bible. Forget the words—the parson came up with something. All cost a bomb of course, but it was the least we could do, wasn't it? Daresay you'll want to chip in.... What is it they say? "The good die young".... Christ, I still don't understand why it happened....'

41

Green woke in a sweat.

Early morning chilly, grey light through the chink in the curtains. He sat on the edge of his bed, not properly recalling the dream but, as ever, it had left handprints on the wall of his consciousness.

He sat and shivered. The whistle had gone from his head, like a departing train. He put on his parka, picked up his tartan case, pulled the curtains aside, opened the door on to the fire escape.

Out there was the half light of dawn. A few stars still littered the sky and there was the sound of distant traffic.

His nerves sang and he had no thought but to get on the move. He closed the door behind him and, with no particular stealth, descended the iron staircase into the new and naked day.

7

The sun was out, slowly drying the streets but the wind persisted, sucking in and out of doorways.

Green's brain functioned according to mysterious laws of its own, guiding his feet round those right hand corners, tramping out the pattern of a maze. Destination and purpose lurked always just out of reach: there was a sheet of frosted glass, as it were, dividing two halves of his consciousness. Sometimes cracks appeared, at others a random incident or sudden shock would fly out of nowhere and threaten to shatter it like a stone.

No casual passer-by noticed anything particularly odd about Green. He was a little tipsy, perhaps, even so early in the day—or he hadn't yet fully recovered from an injury or illness. And, for Green's part, in the first stages of his strange odyssey, he was able to keep the scattered furniture of his mind stored away under dust sheets. In this state he registered his own needs, made sensible decisions between various alternatives.

His feet ached. For some forgotten reason one leg wearied quicker than the other. He grew hungry. He thought of breakfast.

Green paused at a newsagents and bought a couple of papers, one national, one local. Then he turned into

43

a small café beginning to disgorge its customers into their working day. He ordered ham and eggs and toast and coffee. Then he occupied a stool by the counter and, while waiting for breakfast, put his feet on the tartan case and scanned the papers.

Headlines: politics, bombs in Belfast, the latest crop of strikes. He read with fluency and understanding. He turned to the sports pages.

His breakfast arrived. Green nibbled at a piece of toast, then turned to the local newspaper. He needed digs and a job of some sort. His eyes ran down a short list headed *Accommodation*.

A street map would help—he'd pick one up at the newsagents when he left. And where was the nearest Department of Employment?

Green finished his meal and was drinking coffee when the unease returned—some important link in the breakfast chain was missing.... The empty crockery misted over for a second and he felt a wave of nausea and giddiness but this passed quickly.

He left the daily paper on the counter but folded the local one and squeezed it into a pocket. He paid his bill, forgot his case, left the café, went back for the case.

He bought the street map and walked on a short way, limping along the jostling pavement. He took note of the name of the street.

The wind sighed away, the sun brightened. Green found a seat near a bus stop, took out the paper. He had nothing to write with, so he made identations with his thumbnail, marking one or two promising addresses, not far off, from the *Accommodation* list.

A first call was enough. It was an old tenement house of past gentility, with cracked steps, a wide, thick door

44

and chaste net curtains across a bay window.

A pleasant, not unfriendly woman responded to Green's ring. She was stout-aproned, bespectacled eyes careful rather than supicious. 'Did you say, art student? I hope you haven't been thrown out of somewhere!'

'There was a fire at the hostel.'

'Somebody smoking in bed I suppose!' Green's tartan case apparently reassured her. 'I have a few vacancies. Nearly everybody else here is a student. You'd better come in and look round. Twelve pounds a week sharing, sixteen if you want a room to yourself.'

'Prefer a room of my own.'

'I like a week's rent in advance.'

Green reached for his back pocket.

She said, 'Hadn't you better have a look at the room first?'

'Okay.'

It was nothing special, just a room near the top of the house. Trim, clean, spare. There was a small, flat desk with empty bookshelves above, a single window with flowery curtains overlooking rooftops. Pigeons cooed outside.

Green nodded. 'Fine.'

'What about your books and things?' A first touch of curiosity, a closer look at Green. 'Where are you from?'

'Birmingham.'

'Art college you said? I thought the term had started.'

'Mine hasn't.' Green counted out sixteen pounds into her hand.

She said, 'There's a book downstairs by the telephone. Fill in your details please. I've got a couple of other boys from the art school; perhaps you know them. We all eat together in the dining room. Not many

45

rules. I don't mind girl friends, within reason. You pay for breakages and damage and if you've got a radio, please keep the volume down.'

Green heard a door close downstairs. He glanced round the bare room, grasped his case, went down and let himself out at the front.

He didn't know whether or not he'd return, nor that within an hour he'd have forgotten ever calling there. It was as if taking any step, ticking off any item from his mental list, was quite sufficient unto itself—it required no logical extension.

The whistle was in his head again. He moved off along a street he'd already traversed three times. More slowly now, as if his feet were climbing up the ladder of the hours.

He blacked out.

It was noon before he was aware of his surroundings again. He found a pub. He pondered the bottles on their dispensers, felt sick, bought himself a coke and a new packet of tobacco.

He carried them to a distant table. Brain in working order again, perforated by inconsequential recollections making small holes like laser beams.

There was something wrong, Green thought. Something about drugs. They'd always said...they'd always said....

Back in the sun he regained control. He suddenly knew what came next. A bunch of school kids were being shepherded across the street at the traffic lights and a man with a barrow was sweeping the gutter.

Green asked, 'Can you tell me where the nearest labour exchange is?'

'I ought to, mate. I spend most of my bleeding life there!'

The waiting room had steel chairs. An assortment of people lounged on seats, shuffling newspapers or staring into vacancy. Eventually he was invited to fill in a form.

Some time later Green's name came up. He went into a cubicle, taking the form with him.

The official was a thin, bald man with steel glasses and a benign school master's manner. He scanned the form. 'D. Green,' he said. He shoved it back. 'Better make it your full name, lad. Full address, too.'

Green borrowed a ball pen. His hand shook. The clerk noticed. Green scratched out the 'D' and wrote *David* over the top. He'd written *Hogg Street*, the first name that had filtered into his mind. Birmingham. Number twenty-two.

He slid the form back and the clerk gave it a second reading. 'What made you come down from Birmingham?'

'Art school. Course doesn't start, yet.'

'So all you want is something temporary?'

'Just a couple of weeks.'

'Run out of money?'

'I lost most of it in the fire.'

'What fire?'

'At home.'

Eyes fixed on Green, now. Something wrong, here! 'You had your fare to London?'

'Pardon?'

'Your fare—or did you hitch?'

'Hitched.'

The clerk retrieved his ball pen, looked quizzically at

the revised form. 'Details of any previous employment? Your P.60?'

'Come again?'

'Proof, of identity—you can't sign on here without it.'

'Lost in the fire,' said Green.

'I see... it might have been possible to make you some payment, just to tide you over, but if you haven't any identification.... Look, why not pop back home? If you hitched here, you could hitch back. Department in Birmingham would help, if your papers were destroyed. A fire, you said? Where are you living at the moment?'

'Digs.'

The clerk's eyes dropped back to the form. 'You didn't put that down.'

'Didn't I?'

'I could put you in touch with Citizens' Advice. Or the police might be helpful.'

Green turned away without a word, picking up his case. The clerk's specs took on an extra shine.

He watched the slight, bearded figure stumble out of the cubicle, locate the wrong door, find the right one. He got the case entangled in his legs on the way out.

The clerk thought: if he has digs, why is he carting his luggage about?

All sorts turned up here. Liars, scroungers, misfits. You got to know how to handle them. If you couldn't, the regulation pamphlets hanging on countless hooks provided clues.

The clerk watched the door swing to, took yet another look at Green's form, then reached for a telephone.

8

Green took off into the afternoon. Although he didn't notice, the sprawling roof of Euston Station was frequently visible. However, for once he missed a couple of right turns and drifted towards Regents Park.

A host of pigeons fluttered at the foot of a monument. Workers from shops and offices dangled their legs over walls, feeding them lunch time scraps. Green bought a packet of sandwiches at a crowded delicatessen then limped on, peeling the wrapper and eating as he went.

From time to time his brain shifted to automatic pilot, then the world would suddenly haze back. He was in a different part of town, sandwiches gone, heart thumping behind his ribs. Green suddenly remembered about his weak leg—he had hurt it in the crash of course. But that was a long time ago. Why, now, the throbbing of his pulse?

Fear. Green was afraid...how long had he been afraid? And of what?

Mid afternoon shadows were thrown up in a narrow street, concealing something he thought was watching him. He broke into a run. At the end of the street he scarcely waited for a break in the traffic but dashed across. Tyres squealed, hooters blared, then he was clutching the railings of the park, frantically looking for a gate.

Green found the gate and panted through, clothes sticking to him with sweat. He slowed on the perimeter path, avoided occupied seats and headed, away from the zoo wall, into the empty spaces.

Out there he flung himself down on the grass. He felt drained and chilled. The breeze wafting over him smelt of water. He lay on his back, using his case as a pillow, and the uncut grass whispered around him.

It was like the continuance of a dream at the hotel, or a dream within a dream....

The bloodshot eyes peered closer at Green. 'Which one are you? Always was like peas in a pod. You ought to go about with bleeding badges.

'Joke, son. I know. It's in your eyes, see? Well, you're grown men, now. You've got minds of your own. At least, you have. You're the one who always comes out on top. When you were nippers it was the same—you fell out of the tree, but it was him done the crying....'

Green didn't remember leaving the park. He was in a high street somewhere, now. Another crowded pavement with open fronted shops, clothing and other gear piled on stalls with sizes and price labels clearly marked.

Green opened the zip of his case. He helped himself to a pair of jeans, a couple of shirts, some sneakers. He slipped them into the case and moved on—it had been an apparently senseless, motiveless piece of pillage.

He came to a large radio and electrical store. He turned into it, pushing past people ogling things through a cluttered window. A quick-turnover place, cash discount, equipment arranged haphazardly on open shelves. The two or three assistants were pinned down by questioning customers some distance away.

Green fancied the electronic watches. He picked three of them up in turn, tried them out against his wrist, eventually returned two of them to the rack and kept the third, strapping it on—without furtiveness, not even a glance sideways.

Another blackout. Green was lugging his tartan case along a fast road somewhere.

His mouth was dry, head humming, pulse racing again. The case was so heavy that he had to keep swapping it from one hand to the other, scraping the bottom on the pavement.

Green was mildly puzzled by the case. He heaved it as far as the first bus stop. Nobody waited there—it was not yet a rush hour. Green took the case into the vacant shelter and unzipped it.

He couldn't wholly grasp how the things had got into the case. Clothing, a heavy and expensive radio, an electric shaver, a pack of cassettes bound in polythene. A digital alarm clock, a Japanese recorder....

A bus was approaching, slowing tentatively at the apparently deserted stop. Green emerged and waved it down.

A black conductor was issuing tickets to a scatter of passengers on the lower deck. Green got the case upstairs and staggered with it between the sparsely populated seats. He occupied a front seat and thumped

51

the case on the floor.

The conductor came up. Green fished out a pound note. 'Tooting, please.'

'Not this space ship, mate. Change at Brixton, okay?'

He eyed the tartan case. 'Have to put that in the luggage compartment downstairs. Regulations. Not to worry, I'll stow it for you. That way I catch the blast when the bomb goes up. Jeeze!' He added, tugging at the handle, 'You gone atomic?'

'Books,' said Green.

'What else besides the *Encyclopaedia Britannica?* You a student?'

Green nodded.

'You look as if you work at it! Tooting? Got a nephew studying engineering down there some place. Gary Parsons—you wouldn't know him?'

'I'm at the art college,' said Green, flatly.

'They make you read as well as paint?' A friendly shine of teeth. 'So long as you're on the bus I won't call in the army. If the inspector boards us, he might take a peep. Guy's got a death wish.'

Yet another blank and Green was in a back street, again within a stone's throw of Euston. Evening was settling on the rooftops of old tenements pattered with television aerials. Street lights twinkled.

The whine in Green's head came and went like a radio that had been left switched on between stations.

No case. What had happened to the tartan case? Something about a bus....

A very bad patch for Green. The fog in his mind curled tighter and tighter, threatening to blot him out. But not quite yet: there was another of those flashes of sanity, a decision of sorts, an impulse striking him like a shaft out of the haunted street.

The tall house had a brass plate fixed beside the door. Green went in and waited, waited....

'Student. Tooting College of Art.'

'Tooting?'

Not overmuch curiosity from the doctor—yet. He was a grey-haired, soft spoken Scot. And harassed. It had taken Green half an hour to reach him.

'What seems to be the trouble?'

'Headaches,' said Green. 'Nerves, like. I was under a doctor in Birmingham. I came away without my pills.'

The doctor scribbled Green's name on a pad. 'That was careless! What were they like?'

'Pardon?'

'The pills.'

'Oh, capsules.'

'Colour?'

'I don't remember.'

'Have you your medical card?'

Green said, 'Lost all my papers in a fire.'

'Fire?'

'I just need something to tide me over.'

'Not as easy as that, laddie. What was the doctor's name? And address?'

'It was a hospital.'

'Ah!' Eyes sharper. 'If you've recently been discharged, you'd have been sent to your G.P. for any continuing medication. What were you doing in hospital?'

'I was only an outpatient.'

'Let me give you a quick run over. Slip off your jacket and shirt.'

Stethoscope. Heart beat nearly a hundred and fifty. A few other simple tests. Green's eyes—something odd, but indeterminate.

He let Green dress again. 'What college did you say you were at? There must be medical facilities there.'

'I haven't moved in, yet. Term hasn't started.'

'Where are you staying at the moment?'

'Staying?'

'You've never been sleeping in a doss house!'

'Oh...Y.M.C.A.'

'The one in Princes Road?'

'Yes....'

'This is some way from Tooting. Why did you come away so soon from Birmingham?'

Green shrugged. 'Thought I'd see the sights.'

The doctor raised his eyebrows, like all Londoners who'd never quite got round to visiting Madame Tussaud's.

There was a problem here, all right. He couldn't think what to do about it. Tackle that pulse rate, perhaps.

He reached for his prescription pad, scribbled on it, tore the sheet off and handed it to Green. 'Just a little something to calm you down and get rid of that headache. There's a chemist open round the corner. Come and see me again tomorrow. Which Birmingham hospital were you with?'

'Can't remember its name, exactly,' said Green.

The doctor thought, maybe I'd better try and find out!

There was a very small number of innocuous-looking white pills in an oversized bottle. To wash them down,

Green bought a can of strong beer at an off licence. He clutched the tin and limped on.

In some dark place he shoved all the pills into his mouth and drank the beer in one draught. Then he flung the bottle and the can into the shadows behind him.

It was twenty minutes before the furies hit him. By then he had stumbled on the canal. He'd got into a loading yard of some sort, somehow, and was looking down at an expanse of black water.

For a time he was terribly mad. Once he climbed on to a quay below street level. He ran along it shouting, 'You bastard! Where are you?' He flung obscenities into the darkness.

Then he was violently sick, tearing his guts to pieces.

Afterwards he stood there sobbing aloud, obsessed by the oily surface of the canal. Then, trembling wretch though he was, an awful clarity swept through his mind like a wind. For a little while he *knew,* he *remembered.*

Now Green was in a pub, hugging a half pint tankard. He was calm; he thought he recalled having been here before. The juke-box, the pattern of lights over the bar.

Someone came in, someone Green didn't know but was expecting. Tallish, clean-faced, young.

He braced himself for the encounter, remembering the telephone kiosk he'd clawed at after running back from the canal.

'Dave? I'm Keith. Glad you gave us a ring. What's that poison you're drinking?' Keith, from the Samaritans, made his way to the bar and ordered a couple of halves. He managed to keep a discreet eye on the figure crouched over the dim table.

So far so good. At least the chap had stayed put. Sometimes they didn't even turn up. The phone call would be merely a random cry from an urban jungle inhabited by the desperate, the lonely, the fugitive, the mentally damaged, the faceless. Or, having kept an appointment, they'd take fright and slip away, leaving you holding two glasses and with nothing more to do than return to the Centre and scribble a brief remark on an otherwise blank report sheet.

Keith carried back the tankards. The washed out face was concentrated on a tobacco tin, the fingers shakily shredding the contents, thumb picking at a packet of cigarette papers. His nails were filthy and bitten short.

'Cheers,' said Keith.

The tangled beard jerked up. 'Yeah. Ta.'

Two or three years younger than himself, Keith decided. Eyes on his own for a moment before switching away, then swimming like two white fish in the shadows of the bar ceiling.

Drugs? Alcohol? No point in making guesses, yet. And you didn't ask. The battered cigarette smelt harmless and he'd requested only a small beer.

Keith nudged his white helmet under the table, unzipped his jacket, loosened his scarf.

Small talk. 'Not a bad pub, this. Forgot to ask if you wanted anything to eat. A few sandwiches left.'

'No, thanks.'

The fag had gutted out already. Green tried to relight it, breaking two matches on the box. Keith fished out the lighter he rarely used and snapped on the flame.

Green nodded, sucked in a mouthful of smoke, hooked his fingers round the handle of the tankard.

56

The eyes swam back. 'Look, I shouldn't have bothered you.'

'No bother, mate,' said Keith. 'All part of the service.'

Green was perking up a bit. A faint smile parted his beard but left his eyes adrift. 'I meant to phone the fire brigade but my finger slipped.'

Keith played him along. 'Just your bad luck, getting me instead of a spare bird up in Park Lane.'

Green clutched at his glass. 'Read about you lot somewhere. Is it right that anything you're told is in confidence?'

'Sure.'

'I mean, just trying it for size, like, suppose... suppose somebody's committed a crime and they tell you, instead of the police. What happens?'

Keith answered carefully. 'Might depend, mate. If you'd just buried somebody in the roadworks, that could be tricky. Even then we can be helpful. For instance, we've a legal beagle on tap, bloke who knows the ropes. How to smooth the way, make sure nobody gets beaten up with a pickaxe handle. All that jazz.'

Green sipped at his glass, eyes steadier and brighter on Keith. 'Who pays for that lot?'

'Voluntary. Well, up to a point. He knows a few short cuts, fixing free legal aid and so on.' He nearly added: so long as the client comes clean and doesn't arse about. But he didn't.

Green said, 'And suppose the bloke had lost his memory and didn't realize what he did?'

'Up to the pros,' said Keith. 'We're only amateurs.' He waited, not sure whether or not to prompt.

A more oblique stare from Green. 'Why do

you bother?'

'Come again?'

'Bother with all these down and outs and nutters. What's in it for you?'

'In my case,' said Keith, 'a cure for insomnia.' But he made a mental note to cut out the wisecracks. All they seemed to do was strike sparks off Dave, like the droppings from his fag.

And despite the jittery hands and shifting eyes there was now an underlying cockiness in his manner, a smirk of thin lips, a tendency to taunt.

Green stubbed out his cigarette and began at once to manufacture another, fingers surer. He shrugged. 'I was only nattering, like. Just interested, that's all. Tell you about myself shall I? To be honest, I'm a bit adrift. Been down here a few days. Hitched from Birmingham. I'm enrolled on this course, Tooting Art School, but term doesn't start yet. I had the idea I'd have a few days sight seeing, get the feel of the big city—never been here—except just the once. Bloody stupid, though. I didn't realize how it would hit me, alone in a strange town. On my uppers, more or less, and things pile up on you, don't they?

'That's what happened tonight. I panicked, got into a flap, suddenly wanted to talk to somebody—anybody who would listen. If it hadn't been you, it would have been the nearest lavatory attendant. Sorry, I didn't mean it to come out like that.'

'That's okay.'

Green had his cigarette going, using his own matches this time. He sucked at it long and hard so that its tip glowed like an orange nebula. 'Another stupid thing, I left my papers at home. Employment card and that. I came unstuck at the employment exchange. I thought of taking a job for a few days—sweeping the streets would have done. No dice, though, not without papers. Suppose I could hitch back to Birmingham and collect them? Reckon that's what I ought to do?'

'What about asking your people to post them on?'

'Nobody there,' said Green. 'We had a flat. Landlord won't take the trouble—he never answers the phone.'

Keith reached for the pen and little notebook he always carried. 'Might be able to help out there, Dave—can't promise. We've a branch in Birmingham. If somebody, on your say so, collected whatever you need they might be able to ship it down. A traveller, say, covering London. Got the key with you?'

'Key?'

'To your flat.'

Green's eyes dipped back into limbo. 'Flat's not ours any more.' Then change of subject. 'Another daft thing, I lost my luggage. Just a case, but quite a bit of stuff. Left it on a bus.'

'Lost property office?'

'Tried. They haven't seen it. It must have been nicked. Don't get me wrong, Keith, I'm not asking for a hand out. I know you people don't do that sort of thing. I'll manage. Just shows, though, doesn't it, how I've mucked everything up?' A nod at Keith's nearly empty glass. 'Another of those?'

'On the house,' said Keith.

'No, my round.'

'Ta. Make mine a coke. I'm with my bike.'

'What make?'

'The bike? Oh, Suzuki.'

'Go on? Nice bikes, Suzukis.'

'You got one?'

Something else off-putting about that stare. 'Yeah. Being repaired at the moment. Have you got a white coat to go with your white helmet?'

'Come again?' But Green had turned away.

Keith watched him head, not too straight, for the bar. He'd been trying to pick up the right signals, but it was like twiddling the broken knob of a radio. By this time, even with a new client, you'd usually got the drift. Often, of course, their stories had gaps wide enough to drive a coach and horses through. With this kid, though, you couldn't even get hold of the reins!

Cardinal Samaritan rule: *always elicit the true problem*....

Keith suddenly noticed the crumpled wad of money under the chair where David had sat. He picked up the notes and was still counting them when Dave came back.

Keith smiled, handing the money over. 'Hey, mate, don't go chucking it about like that!'

'Ta.' Green seemed neither relieved nor embarrassed. On my uppers, he'd said. He simply stuffed the notes back into his jeans, sat down, clutched his glass with both hands.

Keith saw the watch on his wrist. Quartz electronic, a fifty quid job at least. Little extra dials on it which probably told you the time on the other side of Mars.

Green said, abruptly alert, 'Well, thanks Keith. I think we can wrap it up now, don't you? After our drinks, like.'

Keith glanced at the bitten fingers, wrapped so tightly round the glass that he wouldn't have been surprised if it had shattered.

Then the eyes came at him again. No mockery, no brashness, but a deep agonized appeal.

Keith said, not too quickly, 'We don't have to leave it there, mate. Up to you, of course, but give us another ring, any time. They'll let me know if I'm off duty—unless you fancy a chat with Chad Varra himself.'

No smile back. Green gulped his drink in one pull, fiddled round the table, collected his bits and pieces and stuffed them into pockets.

'Yeah, I may do that,' he said. A momentary hesitation as he began turning away. 'Just one other thing I was going to ask....'

'Shoot.'

'Missing persons. Do you lot help with missing persons?'

'Missing persons?'

A small gesture of impatience. 'A list... well, not a list. I meant... some way of... forget it.'

Then he was gone through the crowded saloon. He swung the door hard open and vanished into the night.

9

Green lurked about in the shadows across the street from the pub. He had no clear thought of what he should do next—there was nowhere to go, but this felt of no importance.

The disjointed events of the day were mere outcrops in his memory, happenings and encounters he had stumbled upon in a fog. The people he had met, whether by his own choice or not, had muddled identities and shadowy counterparts to those he had known in different places and at different times.

They had all offered some kind of threat, like spectral creatures insinuating themselves through the draughty cracks of his mind. They crouched in cages, snarling to reach him, and Green's words and gestures—the lies, the evasions, the apparent lucidities; the jibes, the shrugging disclaimers, the counterfeit frankness—these were all lamps which he'd waved in their faces, or fed in bits through their bars to keep them at bay.

Now they were all quiescent and asleep, except Keith. Green was afraid and suspicious of Keith. He was sure that Keith had tried to follow him.

So Green stood there concealing himself until closing time. The pub's clientele drifted in noisy groups out of the pub, starting up their cars or swaying and coughing along the pavement.

Yes, there he was—the figure in a white helmet, astride his Suzuki, cruising out of the car park, waiting at the exit, motor idling until the road was clear.

He stayed there for some time, looking to and fro. For Green? Then he was gone, exhaust smoking at the corner. The lights over the pub's sign board were extinguished. A door slammed, bolts were shot into sockets.

When Green set off at last he sensed someone behind him—the shadow again dogging his steps. He quickened his pace, hugging dark fringes. Now there was no moon visible, no stars in the sky. A fine drizzle fell, misting the glare of overhead arc lights.

His brain clicked into one of its many modes. Could *this* be the stretch? It had about it a bitter nostalgia. Along its curving length the traffic was thick, with headlight beams cutting through the drizzle.

The sudden flare and noise stunned Green. He clung to consciousness only by a hair line. He saw the blue lamp of a police station, fancied himself inside, yielding his terrors at last.

'I tried the Samaritans. They weren't much help.'

'Well, sir, sometimes it's best to leave it to the pros. Now, can you be a little more specific? A description would help.'

'He stole my case. I never saw him very clearly, only his shadow. I managed to shake him off, but he's on this motor-bike—a Suzuki. White helmet. White coat. Registration number KCJ 452P....'

'Glad you spotted that, sir. Very observant of you. Why do you think he wants to kill you?'

63

Green sat on the damp steps of the police station, head in his hands. It was a miracle, or perhaps a misfortune, that nobody happened to come in or out.

Green abandoned the steps eventually, walked unsteadily on through the gossamer rain. He stood for a moment, close to a roundabout where four roads met. He watched the traffic swirl, tyres squelching in the wet.

Green tried hard to remember what he was doing here. He was loath to leave the scene, but eventually his thoughts jumped the tracks again as if travelling too fast....

He was suddenly aware of his body, as if he had just descended out of the sky by parachute. His heart was racing. His head and beard were wet. He wanted a toilet.

Green didn't know how much later it was when he found himself in another maze of dark back streets. A cat miaowed on a roof, a man and woman quarrelled at a high window. Green discovered a smashed door, one of several giving access to a half demolished house.

He groped into a musty passage. Beneath a flight of wrecked stairs was a damp strip of matting where he slept.

Each week Keith did a couple of four-hour stints at the Samaritan Centre. He lived alone in digs and had a factory job where he worked shifts, so his timetable as a volunteer could be as flexible as he chose.

He also took over occasional all-night spells, dozing on a camp bed in the office, manning the phone. Today, however, he'd be off at midnight, handing over to somebody else. Unless he got hooked by a late caller.

One of the wandering homeless, perhaps, weeping on the phone, begging for shelter. You rang hostels or hotels, most of which insisted on full payment or were packed out already. Then you tried the doss houses, if the client was that desperate.

On a couple of occasions, Keith had broken the rules and smuggled a client into his own room. The first was a little Irish drunk whose wife had chucked him out of the house; the second, a kid of fifteen who'd recently lost her parents and had tallied-ho to the big city in search of glamour and got herself molested. Keith had parked her with his landlady.

Rules or not, it was better than telling them to jump in front of a train. Another Samaritan, a middle-aged grocer called Fred, was on the telephone, doodling as he listened to an unbroken tirade at the other end. A man's voice, vibrating with indignation through the headpiece. Fred was sketching a figure hanging from a tree.

Keith scribbled a few cryptic notes on his pad, preparatory to writing a fuller report on the client called Dave.

Birmingham? Accent farther north, but could have moved.

Tooting College of Art? Check, if time.

Hiding something.

Implied he was broke, but wasn't.

Left papers at home, he said. Side-stepped offer to help. Why?

'Our flat.' 'Not ours any more.' Who's 'our'? (Or 'we'? Or 'us'?)

Never been here (London?) except just the once. When? Why clam up? Not important?

65

A liar?

White coat? Some sort of joke?

The final question, face like a withered shrub torn from a graveside. *'Do you lot help with missing persons?'*

Just another nutter? Check with local hospitals?

Sane, though. Or do I mean plausible?

Morning duty, Monday office deserted, no calls. Suffering humanity not yet screaming at the new day. According to the log, no further contact from the client called Dave.

Keith couldn't get Dave out of his head. He'd written up the report and, having nothing else to do, he'd dug it out of the file and was skimming it when Henry arrived.

Henry was the Branch Director. He was just back from jogging, dressed in his track suit. Face rubicund and healthy, dog collar peeping through a gap at his throat. Perhaps he had an early funeral and, for all Keith knew, he'd keep his track suit on, jogging behind the coffin through the lych gate.

'Ah, Keith. How's the battle?'

'Cease fire,' said Keith.

Henry sat on the edge of the desk, one muddy shoe dangling. 'Something interesting you've got there?'

Keith handed him the report and gave him a quick run down.

'Have you checked to see if he's on the list?'

'Yes and he isn't.'

The 'list' was a series of short dossiers describing certain characters—some local, some national—who had at one time or another been a nuisance to the organization. Hoaxers, recidivists constantly on the

66

scrounge, neurotic time wasters—people who were, for one reason or another, beyond the reach of the limited resources of the Samaritans. Unofficially, they were referred to as the L.T.G.s—Leave Them To God. Henry handed the report back. 'It's none of my business, Keith, but I sometimes wonder why you gave up your police training.'

Keith nodded at the sheet. 'Too much of that sort of thing for a start.'

Henry said, 'It doesn't seem there was much else you could do. He must live somewhere, but of course it's always the client's own prerogative whether he recontacts us or not. I noticed your query about making enquiries of hospitals. You meant mental institutions, of course?'

'A hunch. He could be adrift from somewhere.'

'Yes, yes,' said Henry. 'But we're not an enquiry agency. You say he sounded plausible but didn't make it clear what he wanted. I know just what you mean. It can work both ways. I came across a young fellow some years ago—actually he came here. Coloured. Still in his teens. He sat, shaking, downstairs, staring out of the window. He asked me to draw the curtains, said his father had just been shot by terrorists outside one of the African embassies. They were after him, watching from the end of the street. So far he'd evaded the gunmen and reached the safety of the Centre—quite a trot. We humoured him as best we could. Gave him tea and biscuits, drew the curtains.'

Keith waited patiently. Henry had dined out on this story for years.

'He really *was* an ambassador's son, and his father had indeed been shot—not fatally, but the incident made the usual stir in the press.' He glanced at his muddy feet and slid off the desk. 'Well, I'd better be off. Nice to have had a brief chat. By the way, we're grateful for your good work.'

'Thanks.'

The rosy, disarming smile. 'Incidentally, I was checking the log. I see you've had another telephone session with our Hilda. Back on drugs, is she?'

'So it seems. Apparently some bloke popped by like a vacuum cleaner salesman and dumped a few ounces of hashish on her doorstep. Dream now, pay later.'

'A great pity! What did you tell her?'

'To shove the bloody lot down the toilet. I know we're not supposed to offer advice.'

'You think she took it?'

'I wouldn't know.'

'According to the log, she was on the phone for an hour and a half.'

'Well, it's her money.'

Henry chuckled. 'Not for much longer, it isn't! I happen to know that the post office has cut her off for not paying bills. I'm afraid, from now on, Hilda's going to have to make do with postcards. And I've left instructions that, if she does telephone, she's to have five minutes and no more. Hilda would chat to St. Peter for a couple of centuries, with the rest of humanity queuing at the gates.'

Henry sorted himself out, zipping up his track suit. He offered Keith an oblique and impish twinkle. 'You won't mind if I offer you one little piece of advice of my own?'

'Sure.'

'I telephoned in the other day—you remember? I had

to use one of the open lines because the special was out of order. You answered.'

'I didn't know it was you.'

'Quite! You called me "mate". I've been called worse, but would you agree that, with clients, one ought to preserve proper procedure?'

'Yes,' said Keith. 'Sorry.'

10

Early next morning a bright sun streamed through the narrow windows of the local police station, out of what could be glimpsed of a virgin sky.

The elderly station sergeant on duty loosened his tie—the Victorian building enjoyed no air conditioning. He sipped from a stained tea mug and leafed through the papers on his desk.

It had been a fairly quiet night, apparently. The usual pilfering at one of the warehouses by the canal. Serve them right! They'd frequently been advised to replace their locks and fastenings. A kid of six could have opened most of them with a pointed lolly stick.

Some woman had rung in, hysterically claiming that she'd been bitten by a stray dog. (At one o'clock in the morning?) Convinced she had rabies. Somebody had rounded up the beast and dragged it in, at the end of a rope. No rabies. Just semi-starved; the dustbins had been emptied the previous day.

A couple of tearaways were still locked in the cells downstairs. C.I.D. had called by after breakfast, threatening to burn the culprits with fag ends, no doubt —anything for crime prevention.

Another report, near the bottom of the pile. Badly typed, worse spelt. Signed 'D. C. Thompson', of

70

course. When was somebody going to send that illiterate young so-and-so on a course?

The sergeant swilled down the rest of his tea and shouted to nobody in particular, 'Is Tommo about? Somebody get him off his butt and tell him I'd like a word.'

Apparently D. C. Thompson was tracked down in the canteen. There was egg on his mouth. 'You wanted me, Sarge?'

'Yes. What's all this?'

The young detective constable screwed up his eyes at his own typescript and tugged at the button on his baggy duffel coat. 'A report, Sarge.'

'Looks more like a menu from a Chinese restaurant. Be a good lad and steer me through it.'

'Nutter about. Seems to be running round in circles.'

'Don't they all?'

'Yes, but this one is trouble. I reckon he *is* the same.'

'The same as what?'

'One who's up to all these capers. If he isn't nabbed, he'll treble our local crime rate in the next twenty-four hours. Started on Friday, so far as we know. Manager of Multilectrics, in Dawson Street, gave us a bleep. Claimed that about five hundred quid's worth of stuff had been lifted during the afternoon. Appears one of the staff got suspicious, about two hours too late. Then they got round to a spot check.'

The sergeant scowled. 'I thought at those places they kept their stuff chained up or locked behind glass.'

'They've got a T.V. scanner. Not that it's much use if nobody's watching the monitor. Anyway, it was on the blink. I ask you, a radio and electrical shop and the scanner's on the blink! The assistant remembers a young bloke coming in. Bearded, carrying a tartan case. Stumbled out lugging the case as if it was full of gold bars. Assistant didn't, at the time, have any excuse for stopping him.'

'They seem to have been careless.'

'You can say that again. I took a look round myself. Thieves' paradise. Stereo radios just sitting there waiting to be nicked, electronic watches strewn all over the place. It's like leaving the Crown Jewels on a Woolworth's counter, next to the sweets.'

'And then?'

'Page two. Plot thickens. The bearded chap was the thief, all right. A bit later he boarded a bus. Conductor's description matches. Chummy, probably not local—north country accent. Didn't seem to know his way round. Wanted to get to Tooting. Said he was a student at the college of art there.'

'And?'

'There *isn't* a Tooting College of Art, as such. There's this current rule about luggage being stowed downstairs. Conductor lugged it down himself but didn't think it worth checking the contents. Inspector hops on and Chummy hops off, leaving his case behind. It was dug out at the Brixton terminus. Just about everything inside, except a bomb, of course—or the radio telescope from Jodrell Bank.'

'Who saw him skip?'

'One of the passengers. Mentioned it to the conductor because he thought he was fare dodging. No sweat—you don't reverse a double-decker bus half a mile up a main street.'

'Anything else in the case besides the stolen stuff?'

'Items of clothing—new, labels still attached.'

'Prints?'

'Guv doesn't think it worth bothering Interpol with them at the moment. The gear's been returned to the shops apart from anything Chummy may have pocketed. We can always think again if he cleans out Harrods.'

The desk sergeant nodded. 'Well, he ought to be easy enough to pick up. What's this?'

'Page three. Youth with the same description booked in late on Thursday night at a small hotel, just across from Euston. Did a moonlighter down the fire escape, not bothering to pay his bill.' He pointed helpfully at the foot of the page. 'Then he turned up for a third time. Clerk at the Department of Employment round the corner thought he should mention it. Young bearded chap wandered in, asking for temporary work. Had no documents with him, looked sick. Told the clerk he was from Birmingham—art student. Gave his name as David Green. That, by the way, checks with the hotel register.'

'Chummy seems to be getting in people's hair.'

'And he's not exactly a little Marco Polo, is he? That hotel, the labour exchange, the spot where he boarded the bus—all within a mile radius or so.'

'Page four....'

'Thought you'd get round to that, Sarge. Probably not important. Name marked in the case—M. Green. Get it?'

'Yes, I get it. He calls himself *David.*'

'And if he wanted an alias, why stick to his surname and alter his Christian?'

'No address in the case, I suppose?'

'Might have been once. Part of the lining had been

cut out just under the name.'

'Devious! What next, Tommo? Are you going to have all the Greens in Birmingham checked out? Shouldn't take more than six months. Still, you seem to be on the ball. So long as they keep you well away from the clerical department, you should go far. I think we've wasted enough of our time, though, don't you? The name in the case doesn't mean much. He could have borrowed it from his dad or his Uncle Jack—or his sister for that matter!'

Keith turned up for duty on that Tuesday evening and found a note in the log.

There was another volunteer on the second telephone and an enthusiastic beginner learning the ropes. It was easy enough to get away.

Euston Station, the main book stall. So Dave was catching a train back to Birmingham and just wanted to say 'goodbye'?

Keith left his Suzuki chained up behind the Centre. He could walk to Euston in ten minutes. His latest girl friend had jilted him a few months before and Keith had providently sold the second helmet. Besides, being yelled at by a client above the crackle of a motor-bike engine was not exactly communication.

He found him easily enough, browsing among the paperbacks. Dave looked quite spruce tonight. He'd had a wash, cleaned what was left of his fingernails, even run a comb through his beard.

He gave Keith a furtive, not particularly friendly, glance, put the book back on the shelf and strolled towards him with a nod.

'Where to?' asked Keith. 'The bar?'

'Too crowded,' said Green. 'What about the top of a bus?'

'As you like, mate,' said Keith, who had once interviewed a parolled prisoner out of Wormwood Scrubs on the giant wheel at Battersea Pleasure Gardens.

It didn't seem to matter which bus. They took the first that came along, heading south. Not crowded at this time of the evening—it was well off the theatre routes. They sat, shoulder to shoulder, on the upper deck at the front.

Keith fished for coins. Green said, 'This one's on me.'

'Ta,' said Keith.

'Where are we going?'

'Don't know. I think this route takes in a stretch of the river. That do? We can always jump for it, if you like, and head for a pub.'

Green said, 'It's not that I feel like talking much.'

'Fair enough,' said Keith. He picked up a note of aggro.

'That's all you lot think of, isn't it? Talk, talk, talk! Tell me something, *mate*. Do you ever do anything more useful? It's a lot to ask, I know. After all, it is for free.'

Keith took this in his stride. Green rolled his inevitable cigarette and Keith flashed his lighter.

Green said, 'Quiet up here.'

Perhaps he meant dark. The electric bulb immediately above them had blown.

Green drew smoke, his eyes suddenly white and expressionless in the brief glow. 'Do you ever feel you're a kind of human dustbin? Keeping your lid

75

open, like, so that other folk can fling their rubbish into you? No problem is it? Soon as you get shot of somebody, you can always bang the lid down to keep the rats out.'

Keith waited for whatever was in Dave to boil over. There was something different but hard to define. Personality more distinctive, as if he had found an island and was relishing the solid ground under his feet. None of the occasional stammer, or that almost comic way the flimsy beard wobbled whenever his lip trembled. Hands steady, but during the pauses in his monologue the bitten fingers would sometimes beat a silent tattoo on his knee.

'I told you a lot of balls the other night. Sorry about that. I'd been drinking a bit and I was still in a twist. I've sorted things out, now. Well, so far as I can. At first I thought, well, okay, so there's no need to bother anybody again. But it didn't seem straight, leaving it like that. Besides, I know somebody who does need your help. That article I read, though....they have to come direct, don't they? I mean, you're not allowed to take anybody on—on somebody else's say so, like.'

'Sorry...' said Keith.

'Not even if it's my brother?'

11

Keith waited—as always.

The bus trundled on its way, a few passengers getting on or off. By now they had turned along the embankment. Green looked intently out of the window, down to the river, then across at the tall buildings, their lights caught in the water. Some were bathed in floodlight pointing up their individual splendour.

Green said, 'His name's Mark. I told myself I wouldn't bother, when he ran out on me. I said, to hell with it. He can do what he likes. Why should I tag on as always? Then there was this phone call.'

'From your brother?' ventured Keith.

'No, his landlady. That was funny! I'd been sitting in our flat, listening to a record I'd just bought, and then—right in the middle of it I had this feeling. It got worse and worse. I hardly noticed when the record had played itself out. Then I felt sick. I got up. I went to the bathroom. I was sick three times. Mark often made me sick.

'Then the phone rang, just like that, outside on the landing. It was Mark's landlady, down here in London.'

The cigarette glowed furiously. 'I can't remember

everything she told me—something about Mark having been in trouble with the police. She'd known for some time. The silly old biddy was practically hiding him and you know how he thanked her? Cleaned her out. All her rent money pinched from a drawer and trinkets and bits of jewellery—a watch.'

The cigarette burned his fingers and he dropped it and stamped on it with his foot. 'I thought, here we go again. What am I supposed to be, his nursemaid? Not that there was anything new in that. I don't even know why it made me so mad that night. I was used to Mark, wasn't I? Ever since we were kids....

'We're twins, you see? Alike as two peas. Our mum made it worse—dressed us exactly the same. There are photos, us in a double pram, us in a twin pushchair. There's even an indoor snapshot of Mark and me stuck in the same bloody playpen, fighting over the beads. She made us go along to the same barber's and bullied him into giving us exactly the same haircuts.

'She died when we were fourteen. Dad went to pieces, or maybe it was a good excuse. Sometimes you need a good excuse to go to pieces, don't you? He skipped it, had us fostered out to some old cow who was only on the make. This had the effect of pushing us even closer together—or so everybody thought. But in a way, the only time we were really close was when we were rolling about in the street bashing hell out of each other, like.'

The fingers drummed. His eyes drifted at the changing shapes of darkened streets. The bus was taking them away from the river, through a dead market strewn with rubbish.

Green fumbled for his tobacco tin again. 'We jumped

78

that foster home at last, found jobs, went to college in the evenings. We both took up art. Mark was always best at it, of course. He covered the bedroom walls with his stuff. Bloody abstracts he painted with his toes for all I knew. Slick stuff, you know? But I'm the one who's got to art school, aren't I? Not him. He chickened out, didn't he?

'But something always kept us tied together, something deep, something neither of us understood. In some ways our minds clicked like a pair of train wheels. I can't think of an example of what I mean—well, yes I can. I told you we had this flat? It bit a chunk out of our joint wages but was better than digs. A little flat, with two beds and a sitting room with a cheap hi-fi we were both paying H.P. on.

'One night, I dreamt of joining the Navy. In the morning, Mark woke up and said, "Hey, Dave, why don't we join the Navy?" I said, "Suppose they put us on different ships?" He said, "That'll be okay with me." I said, "You mean that?"

'He didn't answer. I remember thinking, I know what it is, you bastard. You wouldn't let me go, would you? Where would you be without me?

'Another time he said, "Hey, Dave, what happens if one of us meets a smashing bird and wants to get spliced?" I said something like, "We'll meet the same bird, won't we? Have to find a wide bed!"

'He said, "Come off it! Still, we'll pitch up at each other's weddings." I said, "We can't go to each other's funerals!"'

Green's sparks scattered. 'Then he turned crook—it must have been going on for some time. He started to bring home things—expensive things. There was a

79

radio, an electric razor. I remember having a stupid thought about that razor. This is it, this is it, I thought. He's going to shave his bloody beard off. Would you believe that we'd both grown exactly the same beards? That'll be a start, I thought. Or maybe I'll borrow the razor, while he's out, and shave off my own. I knew I wouldn't have the nerve, though. We'd never bothered about each other's nakedness, but *that* .... How much further does this bloody bus go?'

Keith said, 'We can get off whenever you like.'

'Doesn't matter.' Green brooded for a while, hunched by the bus window, dwarfish, breathing heavily, coughing.

He said, '*And* he was on drugs, did I tell you? Started main-lining—I found a syringe. Then one morning out of the blue he said, "I'm heading for the smoke." The floor hit me. "Go on?" I said. It was in his eyes. The sod was pleased. He was pleased! He wanted us to split up, that was it. He *wanted* us to split. And he didn't waste much time about it. He didn't seem to have any special plans. A couple of days later he packed a case, said he was catching the night train and wasn't coming back. We argued about what belonged to me, and what to him. Not that he took much—only a case.

'That's what made me think he'd come back. I told you, he had a lot of gear—mostly stuff he'd nicked, like. He'd write, I thought, then I'd have an address. Does this make sense? I loathed his guts but I wanted his address.

'Can't really explain what it was like, how it felt— Mark no longer being there. Why is it you can't do without someone you hate?'

Keith let that one go. Green seemed to have dried up,

turning back to the bus window with light and shadows alternately on his face.

Keith said, 'Your brother's landlady—she didn't tell you where she lived?'

'Stupid bitch!' said Green. 'No.' His mind jumped on to a new track. 'I told you I had a motor-bike—a Suzuki like yours.'

'Yes.'

'And you said most things were in confidence? I got as tight as a coot one night. Bashed into a truck, broke my leg.'

'When was that?'

A casual question with no overtone but Green's face turned on him. 'Why do you want to know?'

'Only wondered.'

'Why?'

'Sorry—it isn't important.'

'Then why the quiz?' A drop in tone, a fresh shuffle, a new cigarette. 'They thought I did it on purpose. Silly sods! Because of Mark? It was bad enough living with him without dying for him! It was an accident.'

'Sure.'

'Couple of months back, if that satisfies your curiosity. I'm clear with the police.' An unexpected, unnerving laugh. 'They couldn't shove the breathalyser in my mouth—I lost a couple of teeth. By the time the medic pushed a needle in for a blood test, I'd sweated it out.'

'Fine,' said Keith.

'He knows,' said Green. '*He* knows.... I've seen him. Not that he'll come out in the open, like. Just following me about. His idea of a tease—like when we were kids. He'd hide, make me tag along and find him, then jump

81

down on me from a tree or a wall. His idea of a lark....'

What Keith could see of his face was suddenly pensive, genuinely questioning, 'Say, Keith, when I catch up with the bugger—meet him eye to eye, like— what do I say? *I'm sorry?'*

Even Keith was still capable of surprise. Green jerked himself out of his seat, pushed past his knees, showering them with sparks. Then he was limping fast along between the seats, making for the stairs.

12

Henry, the Samaritan Branch Director, leaned back in his chair so that his feet were a couple of inches off the floor.

He had been listening to Keith with his hands behind his head, eyes bright and direct, mouth broad, brow profound. No clerical collar tonight, but a neatly ironed shirt and a brown suede jacket which fitted just a little too tightly, like something he'd picked up at a preview of one of his jumble sales.

'This brother—you think he exists?'

'Yes, well, probably. If not, he's the fantasy of the century.'

'But he—that is, Dave—didn't press you further to contrive a meeting?'

Keith shook his head. 'I think that was just an excuse to talk about him. And I'm pretty sure, now, that Dave *is* on the loose from somewhere.'

One of Henry's sardonic, compassionate smiles. 'The *loose* or the *run?* Were you thinking of Dartmoor or Broadmoor? Recently there has been a tendency to set up a transfer market! If you're sick of mind, keep out of trouble—there are a few magistrates about quite capable of sending you to jug. Should you, on the other hand, be a professional safe cracker with enough loot stashed away to buy yourself a good psychiatrist, with luck you'll find yourself watching colour T.V. in a private clinic. I daresay I exaggerate.'

Henry was not cynical. The bland masquerade of indifference was a mask of self preservation; too much emotion blurred any path to salvation.

He went on: 'I daresay he'll be back—unless somebody else gets him first. Remember, it's entirely up to him. We're Samaritans, Keith, rather than shepherds. The chap really does have to be lying at the side of the road—or, if he's a sheep who's lost his flock, the most we can do is poke him back through a hole in the hedge.'

Henry beamed benignly at the ceiling. An inspiration, perhaps, for a sermon the following Sunday. He added, 'A suicide risk, you think? The problem is that we rarely can tell. As you well know, clients often use this as a threat—a means of gaining attention. Almost like an Access card! Partly the media's fault of course, not that we can afford to do without publicity. Heaven knows, we haven't much else.'

On Wednesday it was back to the wet. Wet streets, a dull wet sky, cars hissing on the road outside the police station.

Not a good day for trying to read another of D.C. Thompson's reports. The station sergeant picked up a certain zest in this latest offering as if the young constable was coming—too soon in his opinion—to delight in crime and vice and mystery and other people's misfortunes.

'Got to admit, Sarge, he's beginning to get under

84

my skin.'

The station sergeant scowled. 'At least he isn't Jack the Ripper. We never cleared that one up, you know. He's been scot free for nearly a hundred years. What's *this* bit?'

'Page one,' said D. C. Thompson. 'Woman in Albany Place gave us a tinkle. Young chap—an art student, he said—booked a room with her last week. Paid sixteen quid in advance, then scarpered. You'd have thought that, in her own best interests, she wouldn't have bothered to report it. Didn't attach any importance to his disappearance at first—assumed he'd spent that night out on the tiles, or gone to a party. But when he didn't turn up after a couple of days, she started wondering. Wants to re-let the room but, unlike some landladies I could name, she's got scruples.'

The station sergeant said testily, 'Why the hell hasn't somebody picked him up by now? Boys on the beat should have managed it in ten minutes. Tell you what it is, Tommo—all this dashing about in pandas, instead of using their feet, tuning into pop stations on the radio, parking on double yellow lines to pick up their wives' groceries! What's this garbage on page two?'

'Motor-bike pinched. Owner saw it happen from an upstairs window but wasn't quick enough to do much about it. Chummy, of course. Description fits again: the beard, the haunted look. Early this morning. The kid's got taste! Five hundred c.c. Honda, practically new. You could get places on that.'

'Yes, the mortuary.'

'A bit of throttle and you could practically skim across the English channel.'

'Just kicked the starter and off he went?'

85

'Oh, you don't always have kick starters these days, Sarge. Electric ignition. Owner left the key in it.'

'Silly!'

'And didn't get round to fixing the front wheel locking device.'

'Sillier still.'

'Anyway, our lad could have made Clapham Junction in five minutes. Appearance altered, too— even if he hasn't got round to shaving off his beard. Guess what? Owner left his helmet sitting on the saddle. Bright red. And a jacket in the pannier, one of those zippy jobs, all brass studs and a slogan on the back: COME QUICK HONEY. Anyway, Chummy can stop going round in circles from now on, unless he gets stuck in Piccadilly Circus.'

'Registration number?'

'Page three.'

'Then why are we just sitting here?'

'Conversation, Sarge. I've done the necessary before you came on duty. Another panic stations call, with the new details—trouble is we'll probably have to rope in the Scottish police. If Chummy's got himself off his ring road kick he could be a couple of hundred miles up the M1 by now. I've a hunch he isn't though.'

'Why do you feel that?'

'I don't know. Mind you, it did cross my mind that if he's from Birmingham he may have decided to give the British Rail breakfast a miss and breeze off home. But I can't buy that, somehow.'

'Far be it from me to come between you and your intuition, Constable! Wherever he is, he's sitting on about a couple of thousand pounds' worth of angry machinery. He could kill somebody with it—or himself. And one thing for sure, he won't be leaving that on a bus!'

The weather had cleared by evening; one of those calm steady nights, thought Keith, when even the Fates sometimes took a breather.

It was gone nine when the Centre phone rang.

'Keith? Just thought... I owe you a drink.'

'Where are you?'

'That pub where we met the first time.' His voice sounded slurred.

'About ten minutes,' said Keith.

His colleague the grocer said, 'All I get are old ladies grieving over their dead canaries!'

Keith used his bike this time. Green greeted him with a crooked smile, twiddling with a half empty glass— whisky, by the colour of it. He was wearing a studded leather jacket and a bright scarlet motor cyclist's helmet nestled between his feet.

Green said, 'Got myself a bike.'

'Go on?'

'Honda five hundred—a beauty. Been buzzing about on it all day.' A mocking twist of the lips. 'Give you a race later, if you fancy.'

Keith forgot his unquestioning role for once. 'How did you fix it?'

'Fix what?'

'Insurance, Licence... H.P. deal, was it?'

'Oh, balls!' said Green. Beard unkempt again. A familiar combination of swagger and uneasiness. He drained his glass and pushed it across the table.

A pound note came with it. Green said, 'Make that a double, will you? Buy yourself a packet of peanuts. I don't want to hang around the bar.'

Why in particular?

Keith took the money and the glass. He didn't think Dave would notice, so he ordered a single whisky and topped it up as far as he dared with soda water.

Back in the gloom Green said, 'You didn't have to drown it. Well, cheers.' He worked at his tobacco tin in silence before going on, inconsequentially, 'I wouldn't mind doing what you're doing, Keith. Honest, it must be rewarding, like.'

'Why not join us?' said Keith. Any chat was better than no chat.

Green said, 'What, with my problems?'

'No sweat, mate. We've got a bloke on the team who's just been through his second divorce. Quite an expert on marriage guidance.'

Green switched that one off. 'Spotted our old man today.'

'Go on?'

'Tight as a coot, as usual. Mark wasn't with him. I wanted to go over and ask, "Look, what's happened to Mark? I know something's happened to Mark."'

'See how you felt.'

The eyes burned. 'Why the hell should you care what I felt? Mark's been piddling around all week on that bloody Suzuki of his, hasn't he?—trying to keep one jump ahead. Well, I've got the edge on him now. If I wanted, I could run him clean off the road. That stretch of motorway down from the station....'

'Not a motorway,' said Keith, gently.

'Pretty fast strip, though, right? There's that bit where the roads join—no crash barriers.'

Keith didn't see any point in echoing, *crash barriers?*

Green drank again, Adam's apple throbbing at the neck of his new leather jacket. 'Lots of accidents there, I bet. Everything tearing about like bats out of hell...and there has to be some reason why he hasn't followed me today, only our dad. I should have gone back—wrung the old bleeder's neck, made him talk.'

Even now Keith was not prepared for Dave's sudden disintegration.

The ash white face, the quivering mouth, that absurd beard jogging up and down, the tortured hands clenched on the glass. Frighteningly sober—or even more frighteningly drunk.

'Tell you about yourself, Keith. You sit there, picking your nose, saying nothing much, careful not to look at your watch too often, wondering if you'll be home in time to see the horror movie. Well, ta. Does it make you feel good inside? See you at the crematorium, eh?'

Green carried off his helmet, like a skull, under one arm. Keith watched the door swing to.

A quick quote from one of Henry's lectures: *Very few of them really want to die. They merely find living a more tragic alternative.*

Keith sat, staring at the door. One minute. Another—too long?

Above the hubbub of the bar he heard a motor-bike engine explode into action.

He collected his own helmet, zigzagged between the tables, and hurried in pursuit.

13

Green's rear light was a bright clot in the artery of the street, heading at first into an area of darkened office blocks.

Keith kept back, hesitating. Should he try and catch up—or merely sit on his tail and follow? And where? In normal circumstances the Suzuki would have been no match for the big Honda, but Dave's inexperience made a difference; and with his damaged leg he wasn't too slick with the gears.

Moving like a squib, though—erratically fast—threatening to take off and vanish into whatever never-never land his twisted mind had conjured up.

Keith kept to the crown of the road, whereas the rider in front tended to zig-zag, hugging the pavement then swerving abruptly out to pass a line of parked vehicles. Keith stayed close enough for their exhausts to crackle in unison, barking back in echoes from the walls of the buildings.

There were several intersections and at first the traffic lights were as accommodating as railway signals letting through an express. Once, though, the amber blinked on fifty yards ahead. Dave ignored it and so did Keith—hoping that nothing jumped the gun from one of the side streets.

Then a clear red. Dave slowed, turned his head, apparently saw Keith behind him and throttled up.

My fault? wondered Keith. Blast! I'm crowding him....

A couple of cars nosed out from the left, drivers flashing headlights and pumping on their horns. Keith had to stop, if only to let the cars get by. When they had crossed, he cautiously nosed on against the lights then accelerated so fast that his front wheel reared a foot off the road.

Dave had reached a T-junction and turned right into a brighter and busier street. By the time Keith had made the turn the Honda was well ahead, but the brilliant tail light was easy to single out, darting to and fro like the trace of an oscillograph.

Another right turn...this was doubling back on their tracks! Keith had seen his own speedometer quiver briefly near the sixty mark when the great shadow of Euston Station loomed ahead.

Traffic thick and fast, now—but not so fast as the Honda zipping in and out of the lanes, the rider's crimson helmet as bright as spilt blood.

The Suzuki screamed on in a chase which had become sheer madness. The Honda was speeding down the broad one-way system approaching the junction; the bulk of the traffic veered left, but Green had taken the other fork. His rear light swung unsteadily right— he was probably half blinded by the vehicles in the upward lane.

He was leaning much too close to the concrete division mounted with arrowed bollards, separating the lanes.

A police car flashed behind Keith, sounding its siren.

He eased over at once, certain he would be stopped. But the white Jag. hissed on. A policeman wound down his window and gestured peremptorily at Keith but it was obviously the Honda they were after.

Dave must have spotted the car by now. The driver, however, was not pressing him too closely but following the bend of the road, presumably expecting that the mere presence of the Jag., in such hazardous circumstances, would prove sufficient to bring the rider to his senses.

They hadn't met Dave, yet!—and neither had the driver of the continental truck and trailer cutting a swathe with its multiple headbeams on the opposite road.

The Honda suddenly leapt as its front wheel struck the division. The helmeted figure pirouetted, spinning from the machine like a rag doll, legs and arms limp in the arc lights. The bike roared straight on. There was an impact, a gun-flash of flame, the shriek and hiss of powerful airbrakes—then a second grind of metal on metal as a following vehicle hit the trailer. The road exploded into chaos.

Keith nearly lost control, went into a flutter, steadied and veered over to the right behind the stationary police car. He heaved the bike on to the reservation and cut the motor. He stood, helpless and trembling.

The Jag.'s blue revolving lights sent out ghostly beams. The crew abandoned the car, one of them passing Keith with an accident board and paying him no attention. Another was running in the opposite direction, running towards a body lying still, face downwards, yards beyond the stopped truck. A second man was gingerly approaching the heap of burning machinery, fire extinguisher in his hands, squirting foam at it. What was left of the Honda twitched and sweated like a dying animal as it was struck by the jets.

A second police car arrived. An overalled man in a beret had got down from the truck and was gesticulating and bellowing at the policemen in French. Yet another vehicle cruised behind the others, a landrover stacked with equipment. More signs were planted on the road, warning lamps flashed, somebody was hurrying along with blankets.

The ambulance arrived from the opposite direction and pulled up behind the trailer. A sergeant, one of the Jag. crew, had time to bawl Keith out. 'What the hell do you think you were doing, mate? Bit past playing Hell's Angels, aren't you?'

'Yeah,' said Keith, mouth dry. 'Is he...?'

'Dead? He was still twitching when I last looked.' Keith's white face softened him a little. 'Freak, I think—impact flung him clear. Reckon he'll be disappointed?'

'How do you mean?'

'For my money it was no accident. He steered straight for that truck. Friend of yours?'

'Sort of.' Keith felt too sick to explain. 'Can I go in the ambulance?'

'Sorry. We'll need you at the station. Let's do our homework there, shall we? Follow us if you don't know where it is.'

'I know!' said Keith. He didn't explain that either.

14

Still on duty, the station sergeant said, 'One of the things I recall about you, young Keith, is that you wrote your reports in a good, fair hand. And in English, too!'

Keith grinned, feeling at home. This time his report had been verbal and brief. While a young constable was typing it up for signature, Keith sipped at a mug of tea, exchanging pleasantries with old acquaintances who popped in and out of the main office.

He was about to ask the sergeant what had become of Tommo when there was a thump on his shoulder. 'Hello, Keith. How's everything at Sainsbury's?'

'I never went to Sainsbury's!'

'They don't know what they missed. If you hadn't chickened out of the Force, you'd have been nominated Cadet of the Week.'

Keith took in the duffel coat. 'Don't tell me you've made the C.I.D., Tommo?'

'Shortage of uniforms! So they've pulled you in? It had to happen one way or the other. Fancy a quick chat? We can use the Inspector's office—he's out raiding a clip joint and my sergeant's got 'flu.'

'Don't let Tommo corrupt you,' grunted the station sergeant.

In the next room D.C. Thompson turned coyly official. 'Been reading your report. Samaritans, eh? Before you check it, anything else you can tell me—off the record? Look, I know about Samaritan rules, but you wouldn't be cagey with me, would you, Keith? This is my first big case!'

'Case?'

'Well what I call the Tartan Case! Lousy joke—I'll explain later.'

'I'm not holding out on you, Tommo. It's just as I said to the other chap—I only met him three times. It was simply my job to let him talk, give him a shoulder to cry on.'

'Like the actress said about the bishop? You took it a lot further than that, though.' D. C. Thompson smiled disarmingly. 'They tell me you were doing nearly seventy on a forty stretch. Naughty, Keith! Nobody seems to be pressing charges—after all, you were one of us. Blood's thicker than a regulation book, you might say. You only knew him as Dave?'

'Yes.'

'Dave Green?'

'Never even knew his surname.'

'Did he ever mention relatives? Anyone he was in touch with?'

'Talked about a father,' said Keith. Then he added uncertainly, 'And a brother. A twin.'

'Ah!' said D. C. Thompson. 'You'll have gathered, by now, that he's been giving us quite a runaround. Nothing too serious, till tonight. Just zany things....' He told Keith about the case full of stolen gear and the other reported incidents. 'You don't look too surprised, Keith.'

95

'No. That doesn't mean....'

'Sure. He claimed to have hitched from Birmingham, right?'

'Yes.'

'You believed that?'

'I wondered. Is it important?'

'Only if we need to contact...well, somebody in his home town.'

'Pretty badly smashed up, is he?'

'He was fairly lucky—if that's the word. The bike hit the truck, but he missed it. Front wheel struck the reservation and chucked him clear. Fractured shoulder blade, broken arm, concussion, dislocated jaw—silly young sod couldn't have fastened his helmet on properly. I picked all this up secondhand from the hospital. You saw how it happened?'

'Not really. I was too far back.'

'You know that Honda was pinched?'

'I guessed. I didn't have time....'

'Of course not.'

Hell, thought Keith. Who'd have guessed Tommo would have made a detective? A few more years and his eyes would turn into light bulbs.

'And he was riding without insurance or a licence so far as we can tell. French driver of that truck is more or less threatening to have us chucked out of the Common Market. Bloke in the car behind mangled up the front of his brand new Marina. Then there's the owner of the late Honda.'

'So you'll throw the book at Dave?'

'Depends. Anyway, it won't be up to me, will it? I'm just the tea boy around here! By the way, they found a high level of alcohol in your friend Dave's blood.

Where was it you met—the last time, I mean? Crown and Anchor, wasn't it?'

'Yes....'

Keith felt even less comfortable. He wasn't inclined, though, to make excuses—especially to Tommo—and mention the one watered down whisky he'd fed to Dave.

The grin came back. 'Not to worry. You weren't to know he was tanked up before you arrived, were you? This father, this twin brother...reckon they exist?'

'Could do.'

'Only *could?*'

'Dave thought so. He had the idea they were hanging about practically gunning for him.'

'Here in London?'

'Yes. Especially the brother—Mark.'

'Mark! And *gunning* for Dave?'

'That seems to interest you. The name, I mean.'

'Just a detail. Tonight, he spotted you behind him, of course?'

'Yes....'

'In your opinion, he really meant to hit the truck head on?'

'I think so.'

'But not because you were on his tail.'

'What's that supposed to mean?'

'Sorry. It was a statement, not a question.' The chummy smile back. 'At least you got closer than we've managed all week. Every time a panda went round a corner he must have vanished down a drain. What about drugs?'

'Come again?'

'You heard.'

Keith knew he sounded stiff. He dropped the 'Tommo', the old pals' act. 'Not in the way you mean. Least, I don't think so. I do think he'd been having treatment of some kind, somewhere. Then he blew—or was chucked out. No, he blew—which means he cut himself off from his daily dose. Don't ask me what it was, but he suffered withdrawal symptoms. I may have it all wrong—I'm not a chemist—but this, and a couple of drinks, could have played hell....'

'This might have been mentioned to somebody.'

Stiffer still: 'Listen, at the Samaritans we are counsellors, not bloody psychiatrists—or even social workers. All I can tell you is that he turned up three times. He wanted to talk—they always do. I hoped that in time he'd tell me something that made sense. But there *wasn't* much time, was there? And I didn't know about his thieving....'

Keith stopped, realizing that after all he was trying to wash his hands of a responsibility—or seeming to.

D. C. Thompson's turn to look discomfited. 'Come off it, mate—who's accusing you of anything? We're supposed to be co-operating, right? Here, take a shufty—just one or two bits and pieces which might give us a lead. We're already setting one or two wires twanging—still interested?'

'Naturally.'

Tommo produced a plastic bag. 'His effects, not that he's dead.'

He spilled them on to the table. Electronic watch, grubby handkerchieves, the familiar tobacco tin. Money—still nearly fifty pounds. Other bits and pieces of no consequence—and then the railway ticket.

The detective waited for Keith to peer at it. Keith

98

said, 'Stoke on Trent! So he didn't hitch from Birmingham.'

'Not if the ticket means anything, and it should. It's been clipped in the usual way, so he must have been on that train. Six days ago.'

Then he moved to a littered shelf, pulled down a tartan case and opened it. There was nothing in it.

'*His* case?' asked Keith.

'I'm beginning to feel it's mine!'

'But....'

'The initials—got it?'

'M. Green? Dave's brother?'

D. C. Thompson shrugged. 'We're guessing hard. It's just that before somebody sits on your goofy young client's hospital bed and makes out a charge sheet in triplicate, we ought to flush out his kith and kin— whether in Stoke, London or Timbuctoo. They'll be able to tell us more about him than he's able or prepared to fill in for himself. Otherwise, you see, he stays as blank as a cell wall. And what's beginning to worry us, Keith, is that he *may* have done something else at sometime—something that has to be...gone into. Capable of it, wouldn't you say? Of course, the brother—or father if there is one as he says—may show up of their own accord....'

'How?' asked Keith. 'Unless they read next week's local paper. Otherwise, how are you going to check on every Green passing through London?'

'Et tu, Brute?'

'What's that?'

'Skip it!' Tommo looked tired. 'Anyway, why do I care?'

Keith said, 'But you do apparently. Hospitals and

places in Stoke....'

'Yeah. We'll work on it, but have you any idea how many institutions there are within, say a twenty mile radius? *And* some of the smaller units aren't even listed. *And* note the address cut out of the case's lining—chummy, that is Dave, *could* have hitched after all, from anywhere, running out of transport and catching the train from Stoke.'

'Isn't that being...over pessimistic?'

'Maybe,' conceded Tommo. 'Policeman's hazard, as you'd have found out if you'd stayed with us. Pubs are still open, just. Stand me a half pint?'

'Who's corrupting who?' asked Keith, relenting.

15

Keith, the following evening, located Dave in the surgical ward of the local hospital. He had to be shown because the figure in the bed was totally unrecognizable.

This was not due to the extent of the injuries: left arm and shoulder in plaster, a light dressing on his forehead, both eyes puffed and blackened. More startling was that whoever had skilfully reset his jaw had, not unreasonably, removed the beard first. Green had a new and fragile look of boyish innocence. And he was awake.

Keith laid his bunch of flowers on the locker. Damn stupid convention, he decided. He should have brought Dave a cigarette machine which he could work with one hand.

A pretty nurse came along to deal with the flowers— late daffodils and anemones picked up from a stall outside.

Green said through clenched teeth, 'I could fancy her.'

Surprisingly sane kick-off. Keith said, 'Forget it, mate. Bet some young doctor straight off a T.V. soap opera's got a head start. How are you feeling?'

Green still somehow managed to twist his bruised

lips. 'Oh, stick the bedside chat. This your Good Samaritan act?'

'We don't like being called *good* Samaritans.' A bit pompous, Keith knew.

Green faded back into himself. 'When I saw you come in, you know what? Thought you were Mark. It's Mark, I thought. He's shaved off his beard. Just his style, squatting by my bed and gloating, having me where he wants me as usual.' Sudden switch: 'Was that truck driver hurt?'

'No.'

'Bike's a write-off, I suppose?' The grief and indignation of a proud owner.

'You could say that.'

'Police have been in. Lot of bloody red tape. Hell, you'd think they had something better to do with their time. Our old man hasn't been round, then?'

'You think he might be?'

'Yeah. No—he only shows up when there's something in it for him.'

Green fell asleep.

Later that night Keith managed to get D. C. Thompson on the telephone. He used a kiosk and had fed a second 10p piece into it before somebody found him.

'Just wondered whether anything had come up about Dave.'

'Not a dickie bird so far as I know. Enquiries are proceeding and all that. I've been tied up with another case all day. Want to hang on while I ask around?'

'Can't afford it—I'm in a phone box. I've been to see him.'

'And?' Tommo sounded as if he'd cooled off a bit.

'Nothing—except that he seems to have recovered his sex drive.'

'How do you know he ever lost it?'

'And, between ramblings, I think he remembers recent events more clearly than he did. The accident, the police coming to the hospital....'

'Well, he's sober now!'

'That's not....' But Keith didn't argue. Tommo sounded as if he was pursuing a desperate gunman on an escalator—the wrong way up. A policeman's lot was sometimes a snappy one! 'Will you do me a favour and give me a tinkle if you hear anything new?'

'At the Samartitans? Sure. I'm on the verge of a suicidal depression myself. Oh, one little thing I heard ...or did they tell you?'

'What?'

'They're switching him to a psychiatric wing—to-morrow, I think. B block. In the next street. Next time you do your befriending act, mate, better take a hacksaw to cut through the bars.'

The pale man said to Keith, out of the corner of his mouth, 'I'll cover you as long as I can, old boy.'

'Sorry?'

'We've timed the search lights. No reason why there should be a hitch. Dicey, though.'

Keith got away and found David. It was a small, nondescript ward with a dozen beds and secured windows. Not a pretty nurse in sight—just a couple of male orderlies boredly playing whist with up-and-about patients at a trestle table.

David's bruised eyes glared reproachfully at Keith. 'Why have they shoved me in with a lot of nut cases?

103

Bloody police, I suppose. It's what they do in Russia, isn't it?'

Keith had skipped the flowers this time—it was the following evening—and bought some paperbacks instead which he placed by a half filled ashtray. They seemed less worried about Dave's lungs in here— somebody had obligingly rolled him a supply of fags in advance.

Green said, 'Is it right you used to be a copper?' It was surprising how clearly he could talk through a half inch gap of broken teeth.

'I packed it in after a few months,' said Keith. 'Not my scene. I couldn't even supervise a lollipop man.'

'What have they found out about me?'

'About what?'

It was nearly always safe to ask Dave a counter question.

The gaze wandered. 'Did I ever tell you about my brother Mark?'

'Yes.'

'Once, we planned this holiday abroad. Nothing fancy, just catching a boat and bumming around till our money ran out. We even collected pamphlets and swotted up maps. We shoved everything we could into a kitty. A money box—don't laugh, it was just a tin thing we'd had since we were kids. The box had ducks on it, no lid, nothing you could shift, just a little lock at the bottom. The key was lost. We made a joke of that. I said, "We can't nick out of it, like." He said, "Just you try it, kid, and I'll break your neck." Only he was laughing.'

Green fumbled for a cigarette and Keith lit it. 'Then I got home one afternoon and you know what? There was the money box, smashed to hell—he must have used a hammer and chisel on it. Money all gone, bloody note under what was left of the box. Want to know what it said? I'll tell you what it said. It said, "*Sorry kid. Couldn't seem to tell you before. I've got this place at art college down in London and need some cash. Don't cry, will pay you back soon as poss.*"'

Saliva bubbled on Green's split lips as he spluttered on, firey-eyed. Keith couldn't think of a way to stop him. 'I couldn't believe it, see? Couldn't bloody believe it—I even went round ripping open drawers and cuboards looking for his gear. It was all gone—it was like having my guts torn out. Honest, Keith, I tried to cope. I tried to think, well, so what? I can live without the bleeder, can't I? We're twins but not Siamese. And I'm free, I thought—free. He's not here any more to chuck his weight around, playing Superman, calling me "kid", trying to run my life for me. I ought to be laughing, I thought. Now I can do things, things on my own, like....'

Green started crying, a small barefaced boy's cry. He couldn't find his handkerchief. Keith lent him one, wondering when the outburst would stop....

Or if it was really *telling* him anything.

There was a bit more. 'I bought a motor-bike. Yeah, *bought* it that time. Mark hadn't got hold of my post office savings. A Suzuki—you've got a Suzuki, haven't you? It was a bit of a heap. I couldn't afford anything better, could I? Not that it mattered—I just wanted something I could tear round on, any place....'

A glassy calm, now, more disturbing than the tears. Keith, who had met it before, had to avoid the eyes. 'Cracked up—on the motorway. Busted a leg that time—reckon I must be accident prone! Spent a few weeks in hospital. He pitched up, once.'

'Mark?'

'Yeah.' Voice suddenly falling into diminuendo, emotions exhausted, concentration like reeds in a wind. 'They let him hang about, painting his bloody pictures, until I told him to bugger off. I didn't need him any more, see? But he'd nicked all that money, hadn't he? He wasn't getting away with that....'

'So you came down here after him?' probed Keith. 'Hitched, you said—from Birmingham?'

A puzzled flicker. 'Hitched? No, I caught a train, didn't I?' A pause which Keith didn't juggle with. Then, with a weary indifference. 'He was waiting, he knew I'd come. Waiting....'

A nurse wheeled a trolley to the bed. There was a light supper, water, capsules in a tiny container. The visitors' bell rang.

Near the door the pale man sidled up to Keith. 'All clear, old boy. Watch out for the machine gun on the north tower. Goon's trigger happy. With luck you should make the Swiss border by dawn. See you after the war—what?'

They shook hands solemnly.

Tommo rang Keith at the Centre the following morning. 'Easier than expected—we know where he skipped from. Hospital outside Stoke.'

'He's being sent back?'

'No, at least not yet. People here are hanging on to him, with full consultation. I gather they regard him as an interesting case. They can say that again!'

'Meaning in particular?'

'Not for the ears of the general public, mate, you should know that! When are you seeing him again?'

'This evening, if I can make it.'

'Look out for Poppa Green.'

'Who?'

'The father in the case. Stoke contacted him at his digs up there—thought their favourite guinea pig might have scuttled home. Obviously he didn't, but Poppa hoofed it down here on the quick. Bit of an old layabout, the sort who can smell a police station canteen at five hundred yards. That's all. See you in court, eh?'

Keith had no trouble recognizing Dave's father. After all, there were only the two of them in the small waiting room. Visitors' time was in progress, but the charge nurse had asked Keith to wait because Dave was still out of the ward having treatment.

Mr Green sat in a metal chair ignoring the NO SMOKING notice and rolling a cigarette. Now that Keith had seen Dave without his beard the family likeness was striking, despite the day's stubble on the man's chin. It was a grey face with bloodshot eyes straying incuriously up at Keith through smoke. He wore a faded blue suit, like something bought hastily on the cheap off a peg in a street market. The striped shirt lacked a tie. His movements had the slow, controlled clumsiness of the perpetual drunk.

'Mr Green?'

There was a suspicious sharpening of the euphoric eyes. 'That's me. And you are?'

'Keith. Friend of your son's.'

'Go on? You telling me he's still got friends? For a minute I thought you was just another bloody nark!'

There were questions on the hang-dog face—people like Tommo wouldn't have told him much. Mr Green deliberated. 'How long do you reckon they're going to keep us hanging about? I popped in this morning and saw him. They let me in, seeing I'm his dad. What say we come back later? Fancy a jar round the corner? On me, like?'

'Sure,' said Keith, checking that he'd brought his wallet.

It was still early and the bar was quiet. Keith predictably found himself buying the drinks—the customary Samaritan two halves.

Mr Green said, 'Beer's not up to much down here, is it?' The tankard emptied itself as if down a plughole. He wiped his mouth with the back of his hand and gave Keith the puzzled look again. 'Where do you fit into all this, son? Me, I'm just beginning to catch up. I've been back in town less than a month—Stoke, that is. When I heard the news I took the night train. Just about cleaned me out. I'm unemployed, you know.'

'Sorry,' said Keith.

'I'll put it on the table, lad. You seem to be an understanding young fellar. I've been away, a three year stretch. A little misunderstanding with a judge in the crown court. Decent barrister would have got me off, but I had to accept legal aid. They gave me some snotty nosed youngster who didn't even know how to put his wig on straight. That's by the by.' He picked up the empty tankard and gave it a crystal ball gaze. 'Pardon me for asking—it's not that I'm on the scrounge and I'll make it up to you—but any chance of a whisky?'

'Sure,' said Keith.

Mr Green seized his new glass. 'Thanks, that's the ticket. A double, is it? Most grateful.' He'd evidently spent the moments of Keith's absence mulling over the things in his mind. 'I should have kept a better eye on them after their mother died. But I had this business in Newcastle, working round the clock. I thought they was all right, especially when I heard they'd left school and taken on this little flat. I used to think, though, they're going to come unstuck. It was Mark, you see? He's what they call... what is it with twins?'

'The dominant one?'

'That's it. It showed up even when they was kids. As a family, I suppose we made a mess of a lot of things. Take me. Business went bust, wife dead at forty....' The eyes drifted blearily up. 'Why are you so easy to talk to, son? I don't know why you're even interested. I always knew they'd split up, sooner or later. Some day, I thought, some smart little piece would come on the scene and who'd grab her? Mark, of course. He grabbed everything in sight, never mind about young Dave. Mind you, I had problems of my own....' Mr Green seemed to dry up.

'Another of those?' asked Keith.

Mr Green pushed his glass across. 'Don't push me, son. I used to be a Methodist!'

Something different about his eyes when Keith came back. It was not merely the whisky, or the squalor of his own life, or failure and neglect. It was something deeper than guilt.

And a sudden sinking into a brooding silence Keith couldn't at once penetrate. Mr Green was like Dave, he thought, in one of his withdrawn moods fumbling with tobacco, twisting his glass.

Keith said, glancing at his watch, 'Perhaps he's back in the ward by now.'

'He'll keep,' said Mr Green. 'Reckon he'll ever get any better? In the head, I mean.'

'I'm no expert but I think so,' said Keith. 'His memory seems to be coming back.'

'Might be better if it didn't.'

Keith missed any meaning there might have been in this. 'According to Dave, Mark helped himself to their holiday savings and took off down here—said he had a place in art school. Was that right, Mr Green? And that was the start of Dave's crack up. He nearly killed himself on his motor-bike—the first time up in Stoke....'

'Hold on, son,' said Mr Green. 'Are you tight or is it me? It was Dave shook clear, not the other way. And Dave who took the money—but only his share. I travelled all the way down here to try and sort things out at the time....' The question flitted through Keith's mind: *how—if you've just come out of prison?* 'And Dave never had a motor-bike....Oh, I get it—nobody's got round to telling you.'

'Telling me what?'

'Am I speaking out of turn? Well, why the hell shouldn't you know? That little bleeder across in the hospital isn't David—that's Mark. David's dead and it was Mark's fault it happened!'

16

There was no leaving the pub, now. People were filtering in, nudging their elbows and occupying neighbouring tables.

Mr Green was huddled over another empty glass. There were tears in his eyes, tears running down his cheeks. His mouth slackly tried to form words but none came.

Keith placed his helmet on his chair to book it and slipped away to the bar for a third whisky—and the usual half pint for himself. It struck him that Mr Green was rapidly becoming a new client. Any chance of steering him, in future, to a tea shop? This way Keith would be stony broke in a month—or on the road to alcoholism!

He had time to absorb the shock and to tell himself how thick he'd been. Dave was Mark—how could he not have guessed? All along, unhinged or not, Mark had behaved like a caricature of himself, yet, at the same time, projected his own personality so that it stood at a distance. In a weird sense it was himself he feared, himself he hated and wanted to punish; and his own image which pursued him and sought his destruction? And he could, subconsciously, only bring that off by assuming his dead brother's name? A strange kind

111

of vengeance....

Trite, of course. At most a quarter truth. One of Henry's mild observations: 'Do resist the temptation to be little Freuds and Jungs. If I had my way, a total ignorance of their speculations would be an essential prerequisite for any one applying to join us....'

Mr Green was blowing his nose loudly into a filthy handkerchief. The new glass cheered him up. 'Ta. Next round's on me.' Then, as if he'd telepathically picked up Keith's train of thought, 'I popped over to his hospital, you know? Didn't get much change out of the head shrinkers up there. Them bleeders never give you a straight answer. Know what? Mark nicked nearly a hundred quid off one of them, so he couldn't have been that crazy! And his keys and all—that's how he got out. Say, what exactly's a trauma?'

'Deep emotional shock,' said Keith.

'Go on? That's what Mark's supposed to have got— when he killed Dave. A length of rope would have been more useful! No, I take that back. Nobody's saying he meant it, though he was lucky to duck a manslaughter charge. Going barmy can be convenient, can't it?'

'What happened?'

'Well, I'll tell you, so far as I can remember. As I said, Mark got too much for young Dave, so he decided to make his own way in life. He had got this place in art school starting in the autumn—he could draw like an angel, you know—but he hadn't let on to Mark.

Mark was in and out of work, going to pieces even then, thieving, messing about with drugs. It cost Dave, leaving him, but he had the guts in the end—not that I'm saying it would have lasted.

'He never even gave Mark an address, only me. I got

112

a postcard from him, from the lodgings he found not far from here. That's when I went down to see him. He seemed all right, except I could tell he was missing Mark, however things had been. Mind you, I didn't know it all, then—how Mark had taken it, how he felt Dave had ratted on him. Mark's got this temper, see, always had. The sort that can last for a week without letting up, boiling on and on like a forgotten kettle. Well, I boobed—I admit that, now. I thought it was for the best at the time....'

Mr Green licked a cigarette paper slowly, eyes dwelling on his task as if it had suddenly taken on a new and intriguing significance. 'I tried to patch things up, went round to Mark—he was still at the flat—gave him Dave's address, tried a bit of the heavy father stuff. So it was a mistake. Christ, funny how something you do, something with good intentions, like, can go sour. Mark was civil enough, for him. He wrote down the address, more or less chucked me out as usual, and that was that, I thought. They were getting to be old enough to sort themselves out, weren't they?

'I should have spotted something in Mark's eyes, though. It was a few days later—I forget exactly when. The police banged on the door. Of course they never told me the whole story—maybe they didn't know themselves. Dave was on this bus on his way to college, and Mark must have been waiting for him outside his lodgings. I still don't know if they met and talked, if there was some sort of argument. Police said Mark had followed the bus—on his motor-bike. He was the one with the motor-bike, see? And Dave, silly little tyke, must have panicked or something, jumped off the bus—it was on that stretch away from Euston station—and made a run for it.

'Witnesses said Mark jumped the pavement, went out of control...I sometimes wonder about that, myself. Anyway, Dave is belting off along the pavement...hell, could he have been that scared of his own brother? Mark hit him square on....'

Then the voice broke and the fingers on the emptied glass turned white. 'For a while they thought Dave had a chance but he didn't make it...there was the funeral. It felt as if there were only the two of us there—me and a coffin sliding behind a curtain. They never brought Mark to the funeral. A pity, in my opinion—sod ought to have been made to face it. Not that it would have done any good. What was he supposed to do—say sorry? How can you say sorry to the dead?'

Keith thought this was meant as a question to be answered, somehow. 'He...Mark...has tried, in his way.'

'Yeah?' Mr Green was only mildly drunk but Keith ignored the twiddling glass. 'Well he's got his come-uppance, hasn't he? Dreams, all dreams. Spitting out at people like you what he thinks is real, head as full of fancies as a rotten apple crawling with maggots! In and out of hospitals, trying to do himself in, or pretending to. Last time, you know what he did? Chucked himself out of a window—his lodgings up in Stoke. Bust a leg. Tell you something, son? He made bloody sure he was only one floor up at the time! And this latest caper, reckon he really meant to hit that Frenchie? Still, how should you know? How tight am I?'

Keith grinned. 'Passable.'

'I usually ask people. I turn sentimental, see? Slushy, like. Right now I'm thinking, all this time Mark's been in hell. Perhaps he's been punished enough. If the good Lord gives him remission of sentence, who am I to clap him back behind bars?'

Keith said, not thinking, merely following this homely piece of imagery, 'It's been solitary confinement, all these months, and there will be no Dave waiting at the gate.'

Mr Green blinked. 'Months, son? Did you say *months?*'

The weeks went by. Keith found a new girl friend, bought an extra helmet again, did his shift work, befriended other clients through their assorted agonies.

He kept in touch with Mark. Mark's body healed. His spirit, he was told one way and another, would take a little longer. Euphemistically optimistic, he decided (wondering if he could say that three times quickly to Mr Green in a pub).

Mark was himself and at least he knew it, now. But he was quieter, much more of a piece; they made him take his capsules regularly then, as a tacit reward, he was allowed to pop in and out as far as the shops, an orderly hovering about, perhaps, keeping his fingers crossed.

As summer ripened, so did the new beard. It was thicker, more lush; his eyes and hands were steadier.

To Keith, at least, Mark never mentioned David.

One day Mr Green turned up wearing a suit that fitted and a tie that tied. He bought Keith a beer!

'Done with Stoke, son. Got myself a nice little room down here. Popped up yesterday, though—called on Mark's factory where he worked for a time. What d'you think? Three weeks wages owing, all that time ago. I made them check the books. Know what I done with the money? Stopped off at the races, put the lot on a horse! It must have been my day—nag came home at ten to one.'

'Great,' said Keith.

'Got myself a steady job, and all. Watchman at a warehouse.'

'You've *what?* Who the hell's going to watch *you?*'

The brown teeth grinned without offence. 'They don't have to worry, son. I'm going as straight as a king-size cigar these days. If they catch up with my record, that's just too bad—I'm not telling them. Met this geezer in clink, see? Expert forger. He used to turn out references in the printing shop. For five fags, he'd come up with a commendation from the Queen on Buckingham Palace paper. Bloke was a genius!'

Mark's court case was brief. He was bound over for two years, on condition that he attended the hospital as an outpatient and submitted himself to the care of a psychiatric social worker. Tommo winked at Keith as if he'd just personally signed a general amnesty.

Keith dodged the pubs, for once, and took Mark for a ride in the country, lending him the second helmet.

No reaction—Keith knew he'd taken a chance. Mark fed swans, sucked a straw, nearly set fire to a small haystack. He talked in short bursts.

'This probation officer, or whatever he is, has found me a job. Comptons Engineering. Pay's not bad, pretty fair prospects.'

'Great. How are the digs?'

'Lousy. Our old man....' He broke off, spotting his slip. 'He's trying to organize this little flat, like. He calls it a flat but knowing him I bet it's a rat hole.'

'You'll move in with him?'

'I'd be daft if I did, wouldn't I?'

Keith guessed that he would, though.

'You seem to be getting on all right with this social worker.'

'He's all right. Name's Higgins. Got a face like a pig. Big arms, waddling legs...they must have let him out of a zoo. Comes it a bit heavy at times. If he pushes me too far, I'll plant a fist in his ugly face....'

Keith made nothing of this sudden vehemence. He'd met Mr Higgins, though—a plump, soft-voiced little Baptist who believed in saving souls. The best of British, mate!

It was early autumn and Keith had lost touch for several weeks. Then, out of the blue, came the phone call. It was a Sunday afternoon—Mark must have remembered Keith's regular duty times.

Mark wanted to see him. He named a local park. Keith got away as soon as he could and rode over.

He found Mark and Mr Green sitting on a seat by the pool. There was nobody much about except some kids playing on swings across the bank.

Mark didn't greet him—and there were no preliminaries. He looked up and said, 'It's our birthday today.'

Mr Green winked at Keith. 'Hell, I forgot. Didn't even give you a card.'

'Twenty,' said Mark. 'We would have been twenty today.' Then, 'I want to see...the place.'

The place? thought Keith. But he said nothing. Neither did he wonder why he had been asked along. Mr Green's idea, needing moral support?

Mr Green took over. Sober, for the moment—mat-

117

ter-of-fact, practical. 'We'll have to catch a bus—Number 76.'

Keith chained up his Suzuki. They drifted off into the sunshine.

It was a five minute journey. Mr Green got them off near a pair of wide gates. There was the name of the crematorium in gold-gilt letters wrought in an arc over the top.

And a stall outside with flowers—chrysanthemums, posies, plants in pots, tiny wreaths.

They brought something each with no emotion on their faces. They went slowly through the gates, past the plain square chapel towards the Gardens of Remembrance.

There were flowers growing wild on grass mounds, a scatter of blown leaves freshened by a morning's rain. Then the spaced urns, each with a simple plaque screwed into a wooden support.

Mr Green studied the plaques in turn. Suddenly he stopped. He said nothing. There was a rose tree over this urn.

Mark stopped. His eyes were fixed on the rose tree. He'd look at the plaque, then up at the rose tree.

It already had a certain strength, a weathered stoutness of stem. Its pink flowers were beginning to wither and shed their petals with the season. The wire loops which had once held its new growth to a supporting stake were rusted or broken away—the tree stood firm and secure. The bark had thickened.

The plaque read simply, *David Green, aged seventeen.* His date of birth—and Mark's then: *'There shall be no more darkness at all.'*

Keith glanced at Mark's face. He was reading the

118

plaque, over and over—his lips moved, but without sound. Keith wondered if he knew, if he understood...that they had lain *three years* in their different graves, their different darknesses.

Still nobody spoke. Mr Green got Mark away at last. He went on ahead through the gates, into the street. He didn't look back. He quickened his pace.

He said, 'Sunday. Bloody licensing laws! Not to worry—got a couple of bottles at home. Bought a nice cake, and all. Join us, Keith?'

'Like to,' said Keith.

He thought of his date, he thought of his motor-bike, he thought of the bearded mask that had suddenly become David Green's face. It shot through his mind, with total irrelevance: *they wouldn't have had beards, then.*

He said, over his shoulder, 'Thanks, I'll try and make it later, okay?'

He left them. Heck! he thought. I don't even know their new address.